HOW TO HOMESCHOOL THE KIDS YOU HAVE

Advice from the Kitchen Table

COURTNEY OSTAFF AND JENN NAUGHTON
WITH ANDREW CAMPBELL

First Published 2022

by John Catt Educational Ltd,
15 Riduna Park, Station Road,
Melton, Woodbridge IP12 1QT

Tel: +44 (0) 1394 389850
Email: enquiries@johncatt.com
Website: www.johncatt.com

ISBN: 978 1 915261 56 4

Set and designed by John Catt Educational Limited

CONTENTS

ABOUT THE AUTHORS

Jenn Naughton, Courtney Ostaff, and Andrew Campbell are the co-hosts of the Modern Classical Education at Home podcast, where they share curmudgeonly opinions about curricula, tips for getting homeschooling done, and in-depth reviews of books on education. As veteran homeschoolers with children ranging in age from 31 to 8, their shared home education experience reflects their own neurodiversity, a ruthlessly practical streak, and a commitment to rigorous academics. They also share a love of reading twaddle, the occasional spot of home remodeling, and knitting more they can use.

INTRODUCTION

In *How to Homeschool the Kids You Have,* three veteran home educators lead you through the process of creating a custom educational plan that works for your family's unique situation and your children's needs. You'll identify your own educational priorities and learn how to translate them into a strong academic program. You'll also learn about what science tells us about how humans—especially young humans—learn, and why that information is crucial for the success of your homeschooling plans. Along the way, your authors share their own experiences and those of other homeschoolers to help you avoid pitfalls so you can provide your children with the excellent education that is their birthright.

Welcome In!

We are long-time homeschoolers and professional educators whose collective teaching experience totals half a century. Together, we're probably best known as the hosts of the Modern Classical Education @ Home podcast, which has been called "the NPR of homeschool podcasts." Our listeners know that we pull no punches when it comes to real talk about homeschooling and that we're always down for a deep dive into educational theory, complete with footnotes. At the same time, we draw on our personal and professional experience to translate that theory into practical advice that real-life homeschoolers like you can use. Grab yourself a cup of coffee or tea and a piece of cake and pull up a chair while we introduce ourselves.

Courtney Ostaff (she/her)

I currently homeschool my two children, ages 8 and 14. I've been teaching online for more than 20 years. In the past, I've taught with Birth to Three, in my local public schools, and for community colleges. I hold certifications in math, science, social studies, and teaching the visually impaired. Currently, I teach classes at an online learning services provider that specializes in working with homeschooled students. I'm also the author of *The Online Teaching Handbook* (John Catt Educational, 2020). Aside from my time as a former board member of the West Virginia Home Education Association, as a licensed teacher I provide annual assessments to homeschoolers across the state.

Jenn Naughton (she/her)

I hadn't even heard of homeschooling until six months before I pulled my kids out of school back in 2001. Now, more than 20 years later, I have four homeschool graduates. My oldest three boys are now 30, 28, and 27, and my daughter recently graduated summa cum laude with her BFA in Studio Arts. My youngest is still at home, and he'll graduate from high school in two years. I have a high school degree and a bunch of college credits. As a lifelong learner, I always have a book within reach. In 2020, I founded The Bookish Society, which offers online literature and art classes. Bookish has served more than 150 homeschooled and traditionally schooled students to date, and we're still going strong.

Drew Campbell (they/them)

I homeschooled my daughter in grades K–2, 4–5, and 9–10, and have worked extensively with homeschoolers as a private academic tutor. I hold a BA in Literature and Languages from Bennington College and a PhD in Germanic Literature and Languages from Washington University, St. Louis. I've been a classroom teacher and private school administrator as well as an editor and translator of literary fiction. I currently develop Modern Classical literature and language curriculum for homeschoolers at Quidnam Press. In addition, I am the author of *The Latin-Centered Curriculum* (Memoria Press, 2006; 2008). I live in Orlando, Florida, with my spouse and our daughter, who is currently pursuing a degree in Graphic Design.

Why Homeschool?

If you're reading this book, you're either homeschooling or considering it, or perhaps a family member or friend has given you this book to explain what they do with their kids around the kitchen table. Homeschooling is no longer the uncommon, off-beat educational option it once was; the COVID-19 pandemic meant that millions of American families were suddenly expected to supervise their children's learning at home. While that supervision isn't exactly what we mean when we talk about homeschooling, it did make home-based education part of the national discourse in ways it hadn't been previously.

So who are today's homeschoolers? And why do they choose to homeschool in the first place?

Over the years, we've talked to many people about why they started to homeschool, and in this section, we'll describe some typical reasons. Maybe you'll recognize yourself in one of these common scenarios—or more than one, as there's rarely a single reason that families decide to homeschool. (These stories are fictitious, but they are based on the thousands of homeschoolers we've had contact with over the past two decades.)

The Accidental Homeschooler

Mary's husband was in the military and deployed for months at a time. This spring, their family was sent halfway across the country in mid-May. The schools her boys had been enrolled in ended at Memorial Day and with all the stress of the move, Mary didn't even think of registering her children for school until after swimming lessons ended at the beginning of August. However, when she called the local district office, she was curtly informed that the local schools had started back the week before. Mary was already lukewarm about sending her boys to this district because of stories she'd heard while her boys were swimming. The other parents had mentioned a four-day school week and most of her neighbors seemed to pay for outside tutoring to make sure their children learned to read. The snippy attitude from the district tipped her toward homeschooling. Many military families homeschool their children, so Mary knew she would have support.

The Pandemic Homeschooler

Dawn was laid off from her hospitality job at the beginning of the pandemic, which meant she could help her two older children with their online school. It was tough because she didn't have enough data on her phone for them to be online all day, and the wifi hotspot the school district sent only worked outside, down the block. Dawn watched her first grader fall behind in reading and counted the dollars in her bank account. Swallowing her pride, she asked her parents if they could move in with them over the summer. Her parents decided that they could squeeze all six of them in their two-bedroom townhouse. They put the two boys in one bedroom, and the 5-year-old slept on a toddler mattress in her grandparents' room. Dawn slept on the sofa. When Dawn got on the midnight shift at the local chicken processing plant, her mother, Cindy, ended up supervising the children's online school. Cindy had taken early retirement as a teacher's aide, but the tech issues were a nightmare. By the end of September, she sat Dawn down to talk about homeschooling the children. As an experienced educator, Cindy knew that the children would learn more without screens in the way.

The Unhappy Homeschooler

Alicia looked at her short, plump seventh grader and didn't like what she saw. He'd come home from school with a ripped t-shirt and a blooming black eye, again. He dropped his backpack in the hallway and disappeared into his bedroom without a word. Frustrated, Alicia decided to go through his backpack. His normally good grades had been dropping like a rock for the last few months, and she was determined to figure it out why. She was horrified by what she discovered inside the backpack. His notebooks had footprints ground into them and slurs scribbled on them. His assignments that had been graded were crinkled up at the bottom of his backpack. When Alicia smoothed them out on the dining room table, she found a social studies assignment that claimed the Civil War was about states' rights, not slavery. Apparently, her son had turned in the assignment with all blank spots, and had received a zero for it. That night, when Alicia talked to her husband about her worries for their son, he brought up homeschooling. One of his coworkers homeschooled his children, and they seemed to be fine. Maybe their son could do it too. As a nurse, Alicia could request mostly weekend shifts at the hospital and teach him during the week.

The Medical Needs Homeschooler

Four hours per week. That was the amount of homebound teaching that Tanya's daughter would get. Born with a complex, chronic health condition, her daughter needed a risky surgery that would leave her bed bound for months while she healed. Tanya's daughter enjoyed going to school, but that wasn't an option right now. As an advocate for her daughter, Tanya didn't want her to fall behind in school, so Tanya had talked to the counselor at her daughter's school about homebound education services. But Tanya knew that four hours per week wasn't enough for her daughter to keep up with her classmates in any meaningful way. From experience, Tanya knew that the teacher would send home packets of worksheets or assign videos and games to play, and that wasn't enough. Tanya wanted her daughter to finish out the year with the skills she needed for the next level in math and to keep up with the Spanish she'd been learning at school. That Sunday at church, Tanya noticed a homeschooled girl jumping rope with the other children's choir members while they all counted in Spanish. She didn't really want to homeschool her daughter, but Tanya realized that she wouldn't be alone. Her church family would help.

The Academic Homeschooler

Rachel had never expected to be rebuked by her son's kindergarten teacher because he could already read, but here she was. When she'd been waiting in the pickup line at preK–3, one of the older, more experienced parents had casually mentioned that they'd prepped their rising kindergartner for the entrance test by teaching them to read with *Teach Your Child to Read in 100 Easy Lessons*. Rachel hadn't known that public school kindergarteners had entrance testing, so she'd ordered her own copy and worked through all 100 lessons with their son. He'd picked up reading without much fuss, and now he was waiting out in the hallway with the fourth *Harry Potter* book to keep him occupied. Her wife, Malikah, had always enjoyed puzzles, and a weekly Saturday night board game time meant that their son had figured out multiplication without any explicit teaching. Now their bright boy was a problem because he was bored in the classroom? After the parent-teacher conference, Rachel and Malikah tucked the children into bed and called Rachel's uncle. He'd homeschooled her cousins, who had attended top tier universities. They'd tried their highly-ranked public magnet school, but now was the time to get some advice about homeschooling.

The Special Education Homeschooler

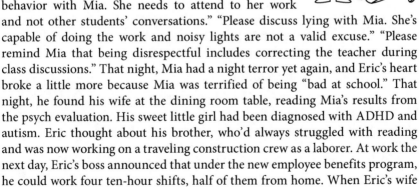

Eric knew his daughter was a little spacey, but she was also bright and cheerful. Or, at least she had been. He watched her step off the school bus with her head down and her shoulders hunched, alone while all the other children ran and shouted. Eric felt dread at the inevitable note from the teacher. "Please discuss class-appropriate behavior with Mia. She needs to attend to her work and not other students' conversations." "Please discuss lying with Mia. She's capable of doing the work and noisy lights are not a valid excuse." "Please remind Mia that being disrespectful includes correcting the teacher during class discussions." That night, Mia had a night terror yet again, and Eric's heart broke a little more because Mia was terrified of being "bad at school." That night, he found his wife at the dining room table, reading Mia's results from the psych evaluation. His sweet little girl had been diagnosed with ADHD and autism. Eric thought about his brother, who'd always struggled with reading and was now working on a traveling construction crew as a laborer. At work the next day, Eric's boss announced that under the new employee benefits program, he could work four ten-hour shifts, half of them from home. When Eric's wife suggested homeschooling Mia, Eric was on board.

The Aspiring-Pro Child Homeschooler

Lucy spent a lot of time waiting in cars and lobbies for her daughter, Olivia. At 15, Olivia was a serious ballet student, spending all her time outside school at the ballet center. Her grades were slipping because she danced every weekday from three to eight, which didn't leave enough time to do homework. Olivia was frustrated because she wasn't competitive with many of the other dancers, who were homeschooled, and were able to schedule their academics around their ballet classes. When Olivia brought home another report card with Ds and Fs, and a flyer for the pre-professional program, Lucy knew she had to have some serious discussions with her daughter. The pre-professional program meant dancing from 9:30 am to 4:30 pm every day, schoolwork to be done after dance. Olivia wasn't quite old enough for it, but she had enough talent to be competitive for it later. Lucy decided to reach out to some other parents to see how they handled homeschooling.

The Religious Homeschooler

Sarah and Michael had both attended private, religious K–12 schools, but a multi-year overseas mission from their church meant that their preferred academically competitive, religious school wouldn't be an option for their seven children, ranging in age from 14 months to 13 years. They knew they would return to the USA eventually, so they wanted their children to learn in English and keep to the same learning as their peers. Both Sarah and Michael felt that Sarah's place was in the home, raising their children. Michael reached out to others who'd been on missions and found that Sarah's lack of a college degree wasn't a barrier to homeschooling their children. Some of their church family had felt called to create guidelines that would help Sarah homeschool their children so that they could eventually return to their private, religious school.

The Intentional Homeschooler

Jakob had not enjoyed his K–12 school experience, and Esteban had been homeschooled. When the couple adopted their first child, Abigail, they'd begun thinking about homeschooling her. Both Esteban and Jakob already worked from home, Esteban as a translator and Jakob as a freelance computer programmer. Homeschooling seemed like a natural extension of the way that their life would adjust to having a child in their home. The couple decided on a low-tech approach in the early years, banning any toys with batteries. Jakob spoke to Abigail only in German and Esteban spoke to her only in Spanish, to make sure she was multilingual. When Abigail turned three, they joined a local homeschool hiking group and began investigating co-ops and cottage schools, but decided that they enjoyed their flexible schedule too much to work their lives around any kind of school. Jakob and Esteban eventually agreed that Abigail would formally begin learning to read, write, and do math when the family returned from her fourth birthday trip to the Grand Canyon.

The Afterschooling Homeschooler

Elizabeth became concerned when she realized that her son, Bobby, wasn't reading like the rest of the children in his class. His teacher kept telling her not to worry, that Bobby would catch up, but Elizabeth was done waiting. She did some research online about supplementing reading at home and learned that many people did afterschooling—homeschooling their child after they did regular school. She joined online groups where people talked about how they helped their children with reading or math, and thought maybe she could do that, too. She wondered how this was different from hiring a tutor or just helping Bobby with his homework, but then she realized that these parents weren't supplementing what was being learned in school. Instead, they were buying curriculum and teaching their children all kinds of things that weren't being taught in school, like cursive or advanced math. Elizabeth decided to talk to her husband when he got back from his latest long-haul trucking job. Maybe they could budget some money for an expensive language arts curriculum that people online said was particularly good for struggling readers.

Jenn's Homeschool Origin Story

My oldest two children started out in school. They were eager to attend, but their school experiences were rough from the beginning. It turned out that, as different as they were, they both had ADHD, one the inattentive type and one the hyperactive type. They were behind in some subjects and ahead in others. School wasn't working for any of us.

I took things one step at a time. First, I ordered a boxed curriculum for both boys for the price of two months' tuition at the parochial school. I thought I'd work with them as if we were homeschooling, just for that summer. We started in June, and it went well.

In fact, we all thrived at home. I joke that it was easier to teach my crew everything than to get them all out the door every morning. I had good relationships with my kids, and they behaved well for me most of the time. My next three kids were all homeschooled from the start.

Meeting Student Needs

As Jenn's story and our other scenarios show, many parents turn to homeschooling due to a mismatch between the family's or child's needs and what the school can provide. For whatever reason, the gap between parents' expectations of the schools and what the schools actually do is just too big to bridge. Since children are usually the single most precious part of a family's life and most people value education, it's hardly surprising that parents will avoid putting their kids in schools where their needs aren't being met.

However, because homeschooling is not easy, family circumstances frequently change, and new school options open up, some homeschoolers do eventually end up placing their children in brick-and-mortar schools, often at the transition to middle school or high school. As we like to say, homeschooling is not a tattoo. It's not forever. Drew's daughter went back and forth between homeschooling and brick-and-mortar schools several times before graduating from a public charter school. The family reassessed their educational choices every year, even changing their plans in the middle of the year when a school situation became untenable.

We encourage families to make thoughtful, informed choices about their children's education, one step at a time. You can only educate the child you have, at their current stage of development, with their unique needs, and with the educational options available to you.

Who This Book Is For

Every author envisions their audience as they write. We think it's fair to describe the imaginary reader we're writing for so you can mentally adjust for our assumptions if they don't fit you.

We assume that you're probably a woman[1] living in North America, with elementary-age children. You're either not yet homeschooling or have been homeschooling for less than three years. Perhaps you began educating at home

---

1 Home education is overwhelmingly handled by women, usually mothers, as we saw during the COVID-19 pandemic. We do want to acknowledge the minority of homeschoolers who, like Drew, are not moms.

because of the COVID-19 pandemic, with little advance planning and little support. Whether or not your family is religious, you're committed to academic homeschooling and prefer to teach using primarily or exclusively secular materials.

You may not fit that profile exactly—or at all—but whoever you are, we want to congratulate you on your interest in homeschooling. While the journey hasn't always been an easy one for any of us, we are all proud homeschoolers, and we want to share our knowledge and experiences to make your homeschool the best it can be.

You Might Not Find This Book Helpful If...

Now you know who we are and some of the reasons we and others choose to homeschool. However, before we go any further, we want to acknowledge that this book won't be equally helpful to every reader. Reasons why you might not find this book helpful include the following:

- **Your children are using online education at home through the public school system.** If this is your situation, this book is probably not going to be useful for you. Homeschooling, as we use the term, implies that the parents, not the schools, decide on and implement curriculum. If your child is enrolled in a public school, even a virtual one, you won't have much, if any, choice about what is taught, or how, or when.

- **You are homeschooling primarily to teach a predefined worldview.** If you're homeschooling primarily to "pass on a particularistic, usually religious, vision to your children,"[2] please understand that this book is focused on secular academics, not inculcating a particular worldview in your children.

- **You are looking for a detailed homeschooling guide with explicit curriculum recommendations.** While we discuss what to teach at various ages and what to look for in curriculum, we do not offer many specific curriculum suggestions. For detailed grade-by grade recommendations, see Jenn Naughton's forthcoming book, *There's No Place like Home: The Bookish Society's Guide to Home Education; The Well-Trained Mind* by Susan Wise Bauer and Jessie Wise (1999); or past episodes of our podcast, Modern Classical Education @ Home (modernclassicaleducation.com).

---

2   Kunzman, R and Gaither, M (2020) "Homeschooling: An Updated Comprehensive Survey of the Research", *Remembering* 9(1) .

- **You are committed to unschooling or other forms of child-led learning.** You should know up front that we are not supportive of child-led education, in which the child's interests determine the topics they learn about. We talk briefly about why we prefer adult-directed education at various points in this book, but if unschooling is your chosen educational philosophy, this isn't the book for you.

- **You are homeschooling as a form of protest against formal schooling or governmental oversight of education.** If you're homeschooling as an "anti-modern gesture of protest against institutionalism, credentialed expertise, and the regimentation of childhood,"[3] please be aware that we are firmly in favor of adult-led education with regular routines and respect for expertise. Although we may not agree with every existing governmental regulation, we recognize and affirm as legitimate the interest of the state in ensuring that all students receive an education.

- **You are homeschooling because your child is an aspiring professional athlete.** We'll be honest and tell you that high-level athletics are not something any of us has experience with. As the rules for participation in athletics at both the high school and collegiate level change often, you're better off getting information and support from a local homeschool group, from coaches, and from parents who've supported children with professional athletic aspirations through high school and into college.

We're Not the Homeschool Police

As co-hosts of the Modern Classical Education @ Home podcast, we've gained a reputation for being outspoken when it comes to homeschooling. You can expect real talk in this book, and you may find that some of our opinions challenge your assumptions. We believe we have good reasons for those opinions, and we always try to bring receipts when we make specific claims. We try to distinguish carefully between our experience homeschooling our own children, our experience as professional educators in a variety of settings, and opinions that we base on scientific research. We also try to be transparent about the ways in which our own varied backgrounds influence our perceptions.

That said, we are not the homeschool police. We will be the first to admit that we don't have all the answers. Even in our 40s and 50s, having graduated multiple children and taught thousands more, we are still learning. You know your

---

3   Ibid.

children and your family situation intimately; we don't. If you see something that makes you raise an eyebrow, we urge you to give it due consideration (check those receipts), but if it really doesn't resonate with you, let it go. We won't know, and we won't judge you. We know that people's priorities, values, and resources differ. The beauty of homeschooling is the ability to be flexible and do what is best for your family.

How To Use This Book

Despite its modest length, this book contains a lot of information. To help you make the best use of that information, we've created a flow chart to show one path you might take through it as you design your homeschool.

One important note: You'll notice that "purchase curriculum" is *way* down this list. This is deliberate. We've seen people spend thousands on useless products because they were taken in by pretty graphic design, shiny advertising claims, or flash-in-the-pan Instagram trends. FOMO—Fear of Missing Out— otherwise known as self-doubt, is real. We've experienced it ourselves. Live and learn from our mistakes.

Buying curriculum before you've settled on your educational goals and homeschooling style is like building the roof of a house before you've laid the foundation—or even chosen the build site. There's a lot you need to know before you spend your hard-earned money on curriculum. **Please take the time to read this book and the few other titles we recommend *before* spending a dime on curriculum.** You will save yourself a lot of time and money in the long run.

1. Read Part I.
2. Check applicable laws[4] and start building your support network by joining one or more homeschooling groups on Facebook or elsewhere.
3. Read Part II.
4. Research curriculum for each of the major content areas.[5]
5. Read Part III.
6. Administer baseline testing.[6]
7. Purchase or borrow curriculum.
8. Create your teaching plan (daily and weekly schedule).

---

4 See Appendix A.

5 See Appendix B and *The Well-Trained Mind* by Susan Wise Bauer and Jessie Wise (1999).

6 See chapter 17.

9. Implement your teaching plan.

10. After one month, three months, six months, one year, reassess and adjust your plan.

How to Use this Book

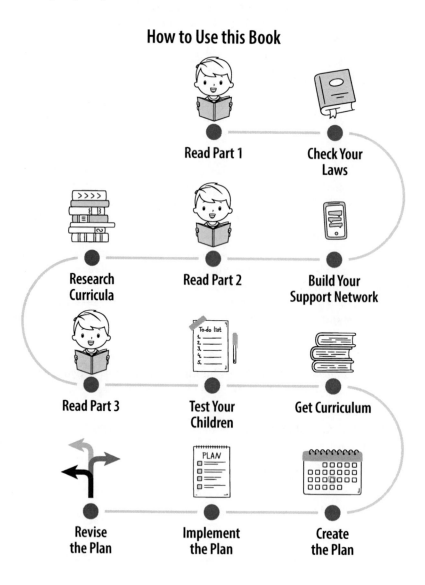

PART I:

BECOMING AN EDUCATIONAL ARCHITECT

In this section, we'll guide you through the process of defining your educational goals so you can choose a style of homeschooling that reflects them. We'll explain what subjects you need to teach at each level of your child's education and how to choose great curriculum that will help you meet your goals. We'll walk you through setting up a schedule and finding a community to support you as you work your plan.

Designing Your Homeschool

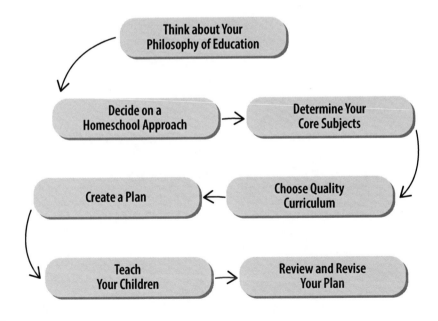

CHAPTER 1
DEFINING YOUR EDUCATIONAL GOALS

Before we begin this chapter, we would like to ask you a question:

What is the purpose of education?

If that question seems too lofty or vague, try these:

What does an educated adult know?

What knowledge, skills, and abilities do they have?

Take a moment to think about those questions. If you find you need more than a moment, that's a good sign that you're thinking deeply. You might want to make some notes or journal your answers so you can share them with the other stakeholders in your children's education, such as a partner, grandparent, or the children themselves. We also encourage you to revisit these questions every year or so as your children get older and their own interests and goals become clearer.

Purposes and Goals of Education

Over the years, we've spent a lot of time thinking and reading about the purposes of education. Here we would like to offer you some common answers to the questions we posed above: What is the purpose of education? What does an educated adult know?

- **Utilitarianism:** From this perspective, the purpose of education is to get a good job so that you can support yourself financially. Since we cannot all follow our bliss into gainful employment, we need to teach our children skills that will contribute to their future economic success in our society.
- **Citizenship:** Here the purpose of education is to become an active member of our democratic society. Students need to know how their government works and enough about various subjects to make informed choices in the voting box.

- **Self-Actualization:** In this theory, education exists to help children develop their own interests, skills, and talents, whatever those may be, for their own use. This view centers the needs of the individual rather than those of the society or state.

- **Liberal Arts:** Here we see the lofty philosophical goal of apprehending truth, beauty, and goodness. Along the way, students develop critical thinking skills, an appreciation for art, and a concern for truth and justice, including social justice.[1]

PHILOSOPHIES OF EDUCATION

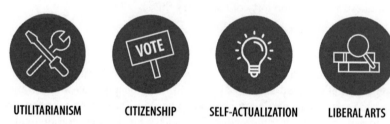

| UTILITARIANISM | CITIZENSHIP | SELF-ACTUALIZATION | LIBERAL ARTS |

You will undoubtedly have noticed two things already. First, it's possible to hold multiple educational goals simultaneously. As parents, most of us want our children to be informed citizens *and* happy *and* ethical adults *and* gainfully employed so they'll move out of the basement someday. Second, in practice, not all of these goals are in harmony with each other. If you believe firmly in educational utilitarianism, you'll likely prioritize practical vocational training over, say, funding the arts in schools. (Two of us are the proud parents of art majors, but… we get it.) If, on the other hand, you hold to the liberal arts or self-actualization ideals, you'll likely fight tooth and nail for those arts programs since they support your goals.

We're convinced that most of the criticism of the public schools and debates about funding come down to competing and mutually incompatible understandings of the purpose of education. In homeschooling, we need to be aware of these competing ideals and figure out how to balance them for our children.

These are weighty concepts; philosophers have debated them for centuries, and eduwonks continue to do so on Twitter daily. We don't expect them to be resolved definitively, well, *ever*, for the simple reason that people are different.

---

1   For a slightly different take on this topic, see Drew's article "The Curriculum Roadmap and the Purpose of Education" at quidnampress.com/purpose-of-education.

But figuring out what is important to *you* is critical for your next steps in homeschooling.

From Purpose to Practice

Once you have identified your personal understanding of the purpose of education, you can start to think about your goals for your child's education and what steps you'll need to take to achieve those goals.

Here are some questions to ask yourself:

- How important is it to you to prepare your child for a college education?
- Does your child have any special talents or interests that you want to nurture?
- What is your family's financial picture? How much can you afford to spend on educational opportunities for your child, now and in the future?
- Does your child have any physical or mental health issues that might affect their education?
- What is the relative importance to you of practical skills versus theoretical knowledge?
- What expectations do you have about your child's independence as an adult? At what point do you expect them to be self-sustaining financially?

Some of these questions may not appear to have immediate relevance to choosing an elementary math curriculum! But they do matter in the long run. Perhaps you believe that once a person reaches legal adulthood they should move out of their parents' home and support themselves financially. If that is the case, you will want to tailor your child's education toward gainful employment from the start, emphasizing practical, marketable skills. If, on the other hand, you are more concerned that your child find a career or lifestyle that is personally fulfilling and you are in a position to allow your young person time and leisure to discover their interests and gifts, then you may not care if they are "launched" by age 18 or 21. You may be willing and able to finance a gap year for travel, an unpaid internship, or even a few questionable business ideas while your child finds their way. Or you may belong to a culture in which adult children are expected to live with their parents until they marry, perhaps contributing financially to the household. Again, this will influence your educational decisions.

If your children are young, you may not be able to answer some of these questions right now. That's okay. Keep in mind that, as any parent of an adult child will tell you, your dreams and plans for your child will have to give way to the actual human being in front of you—who is rarely exactly as you imagined them when you were decorating the nursery. Still, it's worth examining your own assumptions and ideals as they relate to your child's education.

College? Career? Both! Both Is Good!

For the purposes of this book, we're going to assume that your child will need to be gainfully employed at some point. Except for a few members of the economic elite, college is not an end in itself but a stepping stone to future employment, so we will also assume that you want to prepare your children for at least the possibility of attending college. This doesn't mean you have to be "homeschooling for Harvard." It might mean a vocational program at a community college, as it has for several of Jenn's kids and for Drew's daughter. It might mean a state university, as it did for Jenn's daughter. It might mean a private college or university. It might mean graduate school, as it did for both Courtney and Drew.

From this perspective, a college-preparatory curriculum provides at least a preliminary step toward career readiness. We believe that, in the 21st century, any student with the requisite abilities and interests should be given the advantage of a college education. We urge you to choose educational options that keep the door to college open to your child.

CHAPTER 2

CHOOSING YOUR HOMESCHOOLING APPROACH

In this chapter, we discuss different styles of homeschooling. We're calling them "approaches," but you may also see them referred to as philosophies, methods, or styles.

We emphasize academic approaches that are consonant with the college-prep option we discussed in the last chapter, but other styles or philosophies are mentioned because homeschoolers are likely to come across them online or in their local homeschooling communities. Some of these homeschooling approaches overlap with secular or religious *worldviews*—overarching perspectives that provide a conceptual framework and that define the purpose of education for a given family.

Understanding the range of homeschooling options will help you choose curriculum that reflects your priorities.

Common Academic Homeschooling Approaches

There are as many ways to homeschool as there are homeschooling families. All three of us entered the homeschooling world through the door marked "classical education," but there are other rigorous methods you should know about. Here we highlight the most popular approaches with parents who, like us, prioritize academics.

Classical Education

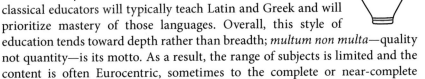

Traditional classical education traces its roots to the ancient Mediterranean world, and it centers the study of the histories, literatures, and cultures of ancient Greece and Rome—or what, at the university level, would be called "Classics." Traditional classical educators will typically teach Latin and Greek and will prioritize mastery of those languages. Overall, this style of education tends toward depth rather than breadth; *multum non multa*—quality not quantity—is its motto. As a result, the range of subjects is limited and the content is often Eurocentric, sometimes to the complete or near-complete exclusion of other cultures. It also privileges high culture: the Western literary canon, European classical music, art, dance, and drama. Most (though not all!) traditional classical educators are Christian and seek to impart a religious world view to their students.

Neoclassical education is based on the ideas of Dorothy Sayers, a 20th-century novelist and playwright. She reworked the medieval Trivium—the classical language arts of grammar, logic, and rhetoric—into stages of child development that roughly correspond to elementary school, middle school, and high school. This style of education was popularized in the 1980s among conservative evangelical Christian homeschoolers and quickly became the dominant style of classical education for homeschoolers. The best known articulation of the neoclassical idea is *The Well-Trained Mind* by Susan Wise Bauer and Jessie Wise. If you hear someone referring to "the grammar stage" or "the logic stage," you'll know they're coming from a neoclassical perspective. Although it started in a deeply religious milieu, neoclassical education is also popular with secular homeschoolers.

Modern Classical Education is an emerging approach to the classical tradition. Since 2016 or so, we've been having discussions with homeschooling parents who are attracted to the rigor of classical education but are put off either by its perceived Eurocentrism, or by religious elements, or both. In April, 2018, Jenn started a Facebook group to discuss the secular charter school line from a popular religious homeschool curriculum provider. That group quickly grew and evolved as members tried to work out what a secular, inclusive form of classical education might look like for homeschoolers. This focus on rigorous academics that didn't exclude religious curricula turned out to be so popular that the group exploded in size, and Courtney and Drew were brought on board to help manage it. Although we no longer run the group, it's still going under the name "Inclusive Academic Homeschoolers." Along the way, we embraced the term "Modern Classical" for our style of secular, inclusive, academic education.

Charlotte Mason and Literature-Based Curricula

Charlotte Mason was a British educator and author who lived from 1842 to 1923. She was a devout member of the Church of England. She was educated at home and became a teacher at age 18. She founded the Parents' National Educational Union, or PNEU, as well as a teacher training school, plus she had an influence on the early Scouting movement. She wrote a series of geography textbooks, an extended Christian devotional work in verse, and six books on her ideas about education. These are the books that explain her methods and that homeschoolers tend to read today. They're usually referred to as "the Original Homeschooling Series" or just "the Original Series." Her vision was "a liberal education for all," which in her day meant not just for wealthy boys. The PNEU made it possible for middle-class mothers to give their children—including their daughters—a broad, liberal arts education at home, either personally or through a governess trained in Charlotte Mason's methods.

Given her support of home education in her own day, it's probably not surprising that contemporary homeschoolers have taken to Charlotte Mason's ideas. Her methods became widely known in the homeschooling community after the 1984 publication of *For the Children's Sake*, a book written by Susan Schaeffer Macauley, daughter of noted evangelical theologian Francis Schaeffer. Although many of the early adopters of Charlotte Mason's methods were Christians, over the years, her ideas have become widely accepted by homeschoolers of all stripes.

Charlotte Mason advocated for what she called "living books"—well-written books by subject experts used in place of textbooks. This has given rise to what homeschoolers refer to as *literature-based curriculum*. Lit-based curricula use living books to teach most or all content areas (math is a common exception). They often make heavy use of historical fiction and topical nonfiction in science. Families that use literature-based curricula may or may not adhere to other aspects of Charlotte Mason's educational ideas, and some are not even aware that her ideas underlie the literature-based movement.

Core Knowledge

Unlike the other methods mentioned here, Core Knowledge is a proprietary curriculum produced by the Virginia-based nonprofit Core Knowledge Foundation and distributed without charge via their website, *coreknowledge.org*. Core Knowledge is the brainchild of the venerable E. D. Hirsch, Jr., who is best known as the author of the 1987 book *Cultural Literacy: What Every American Needs to Know*. Hirsch's ideas—that there is a body of knowledge held by educated American adults and that children ought to be taught that knowledge explicitly—remain controversial, although the concept of a "knowledge-rich" or "content-rich" curriculum has been slowly gaining support in both the United States and the United Kingdom. Homeschoolers interested in Core Knowledge should visit *homeschoolworkplans.com*, a site that simplifies the sometimes-bewildering array of Core Knowledge downloads and provides detailed guides and schedules for each grade level.

Other Approaches to Know

Unschooling

Although it falls outside the focus of this book, we want to mention unschooling because readers are likely to encounter unschoolers in their local communities and certain ideas derived from the unschooling philosophy are common in the broader homeschooling world.

For the purposes of this book, we use the term *unschooling* as an umbrella to refer to educational methods in which the child's personal interests dictate what they learn. Many, though not all, unschoolers prefer learning to happen organically, in the context of daily life. This educational philosophy was discussed in the 1960 book *Summerhill,* and then given a wider audience by authors such as John Holt, author of *How Children Fail* in 1964 and *How Children Learn* in 1967. Sandra Dodd is also another well-known unschooling advocate. More recently, Peter Gray wrote *Free to Learn* in 2013. Unschooling parents typically act as educational facilitators rather than instructors, helping their children gain access to materials or mentors related to their interests.

Religious Homeschooling

Although we focus on secular homeschooling in this book, we would be remiss if we did not mention religion as a guiding force for some homeschoolers. While some on the secular left have homeschooled since at least the 1970s—Drew knows of an intentional community in Virginia whose children were educated

at home before being sent to a private Quaker boarding school—the organized home education movement that developed in the 1980s was in large part driven by conservative Christians, both Catholic and evangelical Protestant. Today's religious homeschoolers are a diverse bunch, ranging from Christian Dominionists (who explicitly teach theocratic principles) to Jewish, Muslim, Buddhist, and Pagan families, representing a wide range of political and social viewpoints. Religious homeschoolers may use almost any of the approaches mentioned here. We've met Muslim families using the Charlotte Mason method, Catholic unschoolers, and classically educating Pagans who teach their kids both Latin and Old Norse.

Afterschooling

As we mentioned in chapter 1, some people supplement their children's school education in the evenings and on the weekends. These folks are known as afterschoolers. Afterschooling often includes academic classes, such as foreign languages, math, literature, and robotics, or it may be limited to art, dance, or music. Afterschooling represents a hybrid approach to home education.

Eclectic Homeschooling

When families begin homeschooling, it's quite common for them to be *eclectic* in their approach, mixing and matching materials from different educational philosophies to meet their children's unique needs. We see a lot of today's eclectic homeschooling parents making heavy use of printables from the internet. Eclectic homeschoolers run the gamut from highly academic to just this side of unschooling. What defines them is their openness to materials drawn from different methods and philosophies. If we had to guess, we would say the majority of homeschoolers are, in practice, eclectic.

Unit Studies

Other families are fond of *unit studies*. In this style of education, families work on a single topic, integrating most of or all the academic subjects. For example, a unit study on World War II might include historical novels set in that time period for English, map work on the movement of troops, discussions of Japanese internment for US civics, and so on. Unit studies often include hands-on projects, especially for younger students.

Online Outsourcing

Increasingly, homeschooling families prefer to *outsource* nearly all their child's education to an online school or to assemble classes from different online service providers that cater to homeschoolers. This approach has gained popularity in the wake of the COVID-19 pandemic as parents sought to provide their children with both academics and social interaction. Another variation on outsourcing is to sign up for a self-paced program that allows children to work online without a teacher; Khan Academy is one well-known program of this sort. Still, other families buy academic materials by grade level on software installed from a DVD, although this has become less popular in recent years.

TYPES OF HOMESCHOOLING

MODERN CLASSICAL EDUCATION	UNIT STUDIES	AFTER SCHOOLING	ECLECTIC	ONLINE OUTSOURCING

RELIGIOUS	UNSCHOOLING	TRADITIONAL CLASSICAL EDUCATION	NEOCLASSICAL EDUCATION	CHARLOTTE MASON

CHAPTER 3
WHAT TO TEACH AND WHEN

Now that you know your purposes and goals, it's time to figure out what you need to teach and when.

Many states or provinces have different required subjects, so you need to determine your local requirements. We've compiled some of the basic homeschooling regulations in Appendix A, but as requirements do change, please be sure to verify everything with your state's Department of Education or with your local district before proceeding.

Core Academic Subjects

Pretty much all locales will require English language arts, mathematics, social studies, and science. We also include world languages here, as some states require them for high school graduation, and we recommend them for students in the K–8 grades as well.

Ages and Stages: An Introduction to What to Teach and When

- **Grades K–3**

  In these early years, your main focus will be on teaching your child to read, write, and do basic arithmetic with fluency and comprehension. Beginning the lengthy process of learning to read is the single most important homeschool activity you can do with your 5-year-old. We recommend a direct instruction phonics program. However, these are also wonderful years for hands-on education, like raising butterflies, planting tomatoes and peas, and creating messy art projects. Math in the early years should focus on work with manipulatives, as most typically developing children work best with a concrete → representational → abstract cycle.

- **Grades 4–8**

  Ideally, the average fourth grader will be a fluent reader, ready to turn from learning to read to reading to learn. By now, they should have memorized their addition, subtraction, multiplication, and division tables. They should be able to read a grade level text and give a coherent verbal summary from beginning to end. Their handwriting should be fluid, and they should be able to compose complex sentences with few spelling, grammar, or mechanics errors.

  The goal of the middle school years is to systematically walk children through a sequence of learning that develops their knowledge, skills, and abilities in preparation for high school. While students' learning rates will vary, an average eighth grader will be ready for more abstract math with variables; writing solid sets of paragraphs with minimal errors; and reading and thinking about challenging fiction and nonfiction texts. Usually, they'll have had a thorough grounding in world geography, a pass through ancient history, a year of physical science, and introductions to biology and chemistry. These are skill- and knowledge-building years.

- **Grades 9–12**

  At the end of high school, the average child will be a legal adult. By then, they need to have the skills in reading, writing, and math that will support them in adulthood—both financially and intellectually. In addition, they need to function as citizens in our republic, which means knowing enough social studies and science to vote well and take care of themselves and future generations. While intellectual and emotional development does not end at age 18, the goal is for your child to be able to function as an independent adult, with all the competencies that entails.

During high school, students need to find an area of focus. They don't always have to do what they love—the idea that they do is a function of economic privilege and not all hobbies translate easily into jobs— but they do need to start the process of thinking about future career prospects and the academic tools they'll need to achieve their goals. Whether that's auto mechanics, nursing, engineering, or philosophy, your role is to provide support, find mentors, and assist with the first steps of a career, including, in some cases, further education.

On the practical and logistical level, you are, at bare minimum, responsible for keeping a high school transcript. Typically, you are also responsible for obtaining and keeping syllabi for those courses and, depending on your state, you will also issue a diploma.

Teaching the Core Subjects

Naturally, emphases in each of these areas change at different grade levels, and the following pages summarize key instructional considerations within common grade bands. In some cases, we also describe subjects beyond the Core Five that can and often should be taught as students reach middle and high school. You'll find more details about these subjects in Part II, where each has a dedicated chapter.

Grades K–3

- **English Language Arts (ELA):** These interlocking subjects consist of reading and spelling (two sides of the same literacy coin); handwriting and keyboarding; grammar; composition; and literature. In public schools, these separate strands of studies are typically integrated, but they do not have to be. Particularly for asynchronous learners, learning to read without an emphasis on handwriting may be desirable, and literature choices might be considerably above grade level. For children with reading disabilities (yes, dyslexia can be diagnosed in preschool), a heavy diet of read-alouds helps them access the curriculum. Beware of accidentally restarting the Reading Wars in discussion groups. Science has established that phonics is the way to go, but not everyone has caught up to reality. Reading is the most important thing you can teach at this age level.

- **Math:** While it has been fashionable to pooh-pooh Common Core math standards, they are not all that bad. Standards are not curriculum, and you should be more interested in the quality of a math curriculum than whether it includes the Common Core. Like learning to read, the Math Wars can ignite heated flame wars in casual discussion of math curricula. The current fashion is for conceptual understanding first, but we are fans of procedural-emphasis math for children with average to low working memory. In other words, normal children.

- **Science**: Young children are not laboratory scientists, and that matters. While we're fans of structured, direct instruction in nature study, don't feel that you need to do intensive labs every week. Instead, focus on expanding your children's horizons through frequent science study, whether read-alouds (the *Let's Read and Find Out* series has been in print for decades for a reason), careful use of family documentary movie nights, or joyfully documenting the seasons around you with a daily nature journal and phenology wheel. Don't forget health!

- **Social Studies**: Like Susan Wise Bauer, we are not fans of the child-centered approach to social studies. This needlessly limits their background knowledge acquisition and gives them the false impression that they're the center of the universe. Instead, go big! Dive into ancient history, spend a month on the Fourth of July, and memorize all the world's oceans, continents, biggest rivers, and highest mountains. If you're feeling ambitious, your children can even memorize how to draw a world map, including all the countries.

- **World Languages**: Although relatively few public schools offer foreign language instruction to children this age (with the exception of English language learners), young students can benefit from immersion-style programs with an emphasis on the spoken language rather than formal grammar.

- **Arts**: Typically, young children are still developing fine motor skills, and the arts are a perfect way to help them do this. Pinching clay, sweeping paintbrushes, threading needles, and plunking piano keys are all ways to hone fine motor skills while building knowledge about the arts and having fun.

- **Physical Education**: Physical movement helps children develop gross motor skills. All children benefit from daily aerobic exercise, and the effects may be even more pronounced for children with neurological differences like ADHD and those with mood disorders.

Grades 4–8

- **English Language Arts (ELA)**: At this age, students can dive into more complex grammar, typically in the course of composition. Their spelling should be good, and they should be ready to dig into more advanced morphology with interesting prefixes, suffixes, and root words. They're ready for independent, silent reading of more advanced books. They should be able to tackle writing paragraphs with coherent thesis statements, supporting evidence, and appropriate transitions. Older children can work up to beginning expository essays.

- **Math**: Ratios are the focus of upper arithmetic, in the form of more complicated division, fractions, decimals, and percentages. Exponents and roots are added in the higher grades, along with more focus on two-dimensional and three-dimensional geometry. Integers, the order of operations, multi-step equations, basic statistics, and the real number system are also included at the upper end of this age band. The basics of personal finance are good to cover as well. Advanced students may be ready for algebra.

- **Science**: Science should be more formal here, and a high-quality, knowledge-rich education will have an emphasis on learning the concepts and vocabulary of physical science, biology, and chemistry. Other areas for study might include programming, hands-on electronics, astronomy, health, and geology. Go for quality curricula over quantities of dubiously effective labs.

- **Social Studies**: World history, American history, civics, economics, and geography are all typical areas of focus at these grade levels. While it may be tempting to just work your way through many of the wonderful middle-grade books on these topics, restrain yourself. Be systematic and thorough, using a mainstream, factual textbook combined with rigorous memory work and explicit connections between places and times. You do your child no favors if you send them out into the world with only an understanding of your point of view.

- **World Languages**: Many public schools begin foreign language instruction in middle school. The most commonly offered modern languages are Spanish and French, but you can choose any world language, including classical ones. If you are outsourcing instruction—and unless you are fluent in the target language, you will probably want to—look for modern methods that include comprehensible input (plenty of listening and reading) rather than an emphasis on formal grammar, even in classical languages.

- **Arts**: If you can manage it, try to give your child some kind of music lessons. Even if your child is simply part of the children's choir at church, participating in music is good for the body and mind. Likewise, a high-quality visual arts program will teach them elementary drawing and painting, allowing them to produce a reasonably life-like product. Remember, the goal is not to produce a professional artist or musician, but to equip them with enough skills to do music and art for pleasure.

- **Physical Education**: These are the prime years to begin team sports if your children are interested. Otherwise, seek out individual opportunities for regular exercise to develop and maintain personal fitness. This age level also brings in more complicated health issues, such as puberty, drugs, and difficult social interactions, and we encourage parents to seek outside support and resources for teaching your children about these issues.

K-8 ACADEMICS

ENGLISH LANGUAGE ARTS	MATHEMATICS	SOCIAL STUDIES	SCIENCE	WORLD LANGUAGES
Skills:	**Arithmetic:**	**Core:**	**Core:**	**Focus:**
• reading	• addition	• history	• biology	• building
• handwriting	• subtraction	• geography	• chemistry	vocabulary
• spelling	• multiplication	• political science	• physics	• basic language
• vocabulary	• division	• economics		structures
• grammar	• exponents	**Key:**	**Key:**	• immersion in
• composition	• roots	• anthropology	• geology	the spoken
Content:	• fractions	• archaeology	• astronomy	language
• literature	• decimals	• law	• health	
	• integers	• philosophy	• safety	
	Geometry	• psychology	• natural world	
	Analysis	• religion	• electronics	
		• sociology		

Grades 9–12

- **English Language Arts (ELA)**: By the end of high school, students should be able to easily complete a short piece of expository writing, such as a five-paragraph essay. A college bound student should be able to write a research paper with footnotes and a bibliography. They also need to think about difficult pieces of literature, both fiction and nonfiction, and do a competent job of writing about them. They'll need four credits in English Language Arts to meet college entrance requirements.

- **Math**: In our current educational milieu, virtually all students need to study at least one year of algebra. In California, public high school graduation requirements extend to a year of geometry. Typically, college-bound students will need at least two more years beyond algebra, and often three more, but you can get creative with those courses. Statistics is a common and respected higher course. Business math, personal finance, and math for the trades are practical options. Again, four credits of math are recommended to meet college entrance requirements.

- **Science**: Generally speaking, students should study biology, chemistry, and physics—with labs. Yes, you can do quality lab science at home. There are kits. In the USA, these three subjects are typically separate, full-year classes. A fourth year of another science is also recommended, and this class can be anything from astronomy to zoology. Some states may have more specific requirements.

- **Social Studies**: Typically, three classes is the minimum and American history is one of those. World history, taught over one or two years, should be another, especially in California or New York. Feel free to get creative with the remaining credit(s). Everything from ancient history to the history of film is on the table. Economics and civics are highly recommended as fundamentals for good citizenship.

- **World Languages**: Not all states require another language for high school graduation, but nearly all colleges and universities do. High schoolers have a wide variety of options for fulfillment, including high-quality online Spanish options that are tailored to homeschoolers. The USA is home to the second-largest population of Spanish speakers in the world, which makes Spanish a practical choice for native speakers of English. However, two years of almost any world language, classical or modern, will meet college entrance requirements.

- **Arts**: High school graduation requirements vary by state, but most colleges and universities require at least one year of fine arts, either practice or appreciation. This usually means dance, music, theater, visual arts or interdisciplinary arts. The visual arts include drawing, painting, pottery, sculpting, photography, filmmaking, and handicrafts.

- **Physical Education and Health**: Team sports and personal fitness continue to be important in these years. Peer interactions and self-care are also key issues. See chapter 16 for ideas on teaching health to students of this age.

- **Other Requirements**: Many states have other requirements. For example, Texas public high school students need a half-credit of speech. As of this writing, New York homeschoolers are required to teach two years of physical education and a half-year of health, while Pennsylvania homeschoolers are required to teach two years of art and humanities. Washington state requires "occupational education." Check your state or provincial laws to make sure you are fulfilling any specialized instructional requirements.

You may feel overwhelmed at the prospect of teaching all of these subjects. Rest assured that you don't have to be able to do so right out of the gate—or ever. Remember how it was caring for your first baby? You may have wondered how they even let you bring this helpless creature home! But you learned as you went, and you adapted as the child grew and changed. The same is true of homeschooling. Chances are, you don't need to be able to teach high school biology next week, and if you're not up for it when the time comes, well, that's why we discuss outsourcing as a valid option for homeschoolers. This overview is meant to give you the lay of the land so you can think about both your long- and short-term choices with the end in mind.

Scheduling

Here's where we get to the nitty-gritty detail. There are multiple options for planning, so let's review some of the key points. Most high-quality curricula come with a set number of lessons. For example, Saxon Algebra 8/7, 3rd edition has 120 lessons. However, after every five lessons, there is a quiz. This means there are 24 days you'll need to devote to the quizzes. In addition, every tenth lesson is a hands-on project. This means that there are 12 of those. Altogether, this makes 156 days of math. Is that enough?

How many days of school are required for public schools? This is more complex than it seems at first glance. Colorado requires only 160 days of school, while West Virginia requires 180 days—that's over 10% more instructional time. How about the number of hours of school? Montana requires only 360 hours for half-day kindergarten, while New York requires 450. That's 25% more instructional time for half-day kindergarten in New York versus Montana. There are similar differences in high school requirements: 1,080 hours are required for high school seniors in Alaska, while only 720 hours are required in Arizona. In Arizona, those 720 hours include lunch!

K–8: Around the World in 180 Days

Given all this mess, our general rule of thumb for grades K–8 is to go by the number of days, and to set the number of days at 180. According to the National Center for Education Statistics, in 2020, the most common day requirement was 180 days,[1] so that's a safe bet. That works out to 36 weeks of school at five days per week, or 45 weeks of school at four days per week.

There are many ways to schedule your homeschool days. Many people "do school" five days per week, tracking their local school district's calendar for 36 weeks. Similarly, many homeschoolers study only between Labor Day and Memorial Day. That's 38 weeks, giving them flex time for holidays. Especially when children are younger, a four-day week is a popular option, giving a day for running errands, cleaning house, and playing games—but since you've cut 1/5th of your schedule, you'll need to study for more weeks to finish your chosen curricula.

High School: Carnegie Units

In high school, a credit is a standardized unit. Developed in 1906, a Carnegie Unit earns a high school student one "credit." This means that the student has spent 120 hours studying the subject over the course. This works out to 40 minutes a day, five days a week, for 36 weeks. Your student could also study for 50 minutes on four days of a week, or study for an hour and 40 minutes on two days of a week. That second option is used by Courtney's local high schools.

Since you're homeschooling, your child could also rotate subjects, studying 24 hours a week (a bit less than five hours per day) on one subject for five weeks and earning their high school credit. Over the course of 35 weeks, they could earn seven high school credits this way. However, since most people need periodic review to remember the content of a subject, we do not usually recommend this method.

Gimme a Break!

What about breaks? There are many options here, as well. Many homeschoolers study six weeks on and one week off, year round. On average, this gives them 42 weeks of study a year, comfortably between the 36 weeks that lead to 180 days and the 45 weeks of a four-day week for 180 days.

1   www.bit.ly/3Qcctha

In hotter areas of the US, many homeschoolers stay indoors and study during the summer, and then take longer breaks in their cooler winters. This pattern is usually reversed by those in more temperate climates.

You may also choose to schedule your breaks around your work schedule. For example, Courtney's children often begin when she begins teaching in the autumn, and take the breaks that her work assigns. Religious holidays form another common break, and those can vary between families.

That said, there are some breaks that many homeschoolers take that we should discuss. In the USA, the February doldrums are a known quantity. Nearly everyone wants to quit in February, with those long, gray days. Wiser, more experienced homeschoolers (and school districts!) often schedule a break in February, to help families get through the winter blahs.

You will also need to build in your own sick days and unexpected holidays. Giving yourself a ten percent margin is generally a wise idea. Feel free to schedule 200 days of school, knowing that you won't use them all. A cushion of free days allows you to take impromptu field trips or binge-watch the latest show while you're down with the flu, without anxiety.

Aligning the Path

Let's return to the 156 days of Saxon 8/7 math. Typically, we would recommend doing math every day. When your student finishes the math course, you could opt to let them relax until your next "school year" starts, or you could do what long-time homeschoolers often do and start the next level. Why? Giving your child a head start lets you take breaks without worrying about falling behind where you want your child to be.

A good curriculum will give you a pacing guide. Many subjects do not need to be taught every day. For example, *First Language Lessons* is typically scheduled for three days a week. In contrast, *Writing With Ease* is usually scheduled for four days per week. Often, homeschoolers choose to take an afternoon for science, because labs can be lengthy. This means that science is often taught only twice a week, but for longer stretches of time. When you select your curriculum, check those pacing guides to see how much flexibility you have in scheduling.

Loop-de-Loop!

Perhaps all of this seems overwhelming. Your child might have complex, chronic health conditions, your work schedule might be irregular, or you have a family crisis at home. We've got you! Make a list of all the items you want to cover, putting math, reading, and writing in there twice as often. This might look like:

- Grammar
- Writing
- Math
- Phonics
- Literature read-alouds
- Art
- Math
- Music
- Phonics
- History
- Writing
- Geography

Then, simply go down the list. What you get done that day, you get done. When you or your child are maxed out, stop. You simply pick up where you left off the next day. Eventually, everything will be covered. The caveat with this method is that you need to be aware that it's easier to fall behind because your days can be very short.

Do the Next Thing

If you have good quality curricula, then this is a relaxing option. Just pick up your core subjects every day and do the next lesson in the book. How many lessons are there? Doesn't matter. You will just keep plowing through, day by day. This can be a great option for the busy parent, and in fact Courtney used this method for the first few years of homeschooling. Different curricula finished at different parts of the school year, and as the spring bloomed, fewer and fewer subjects needed to be done. Very pleasant, if you can swing it.

Spiral Notebook Method

This is a slight variation on "Do the Next Thing." Buy yourself a cheap spiral notebook and find a pen. Once a week, usually on Sunday afternoon, you'll sort through the curricula you've chosen and make a daily checklist of what needs to be done and when. The advantage of this method is that you can prepare your science labs, art materials, and so on in advance, so you're not rushing around during the time you meant you to use for teaching. You can also create the next day's checklist every evening, but we don't recommend that because if you need to skip an evening, then your children won't have their list for the next day. This method has the advantage of keeping a daily record of activities in case you need to "prove" that you've been homeschooling to an outside authority.

File Folders

For parents who have multiple children or anticipate being very busy, and use workbook or text-based curricula, the file folder method is fantastic. Before you start, you buy 180 file folders and 36 hanging files and place them in a file cabinet. You'll put five folders per each of the 36 hanging folders. Because Courtney can be very extra, she used washi tape to color code the hanging files and file folders, so that they were always returned to the correct location. Then she labeled each file folder with Week Number and Day Number. This would look like Wk 1 Day 1, Wk 1 Day 2, and so on, all the way to Wk 36 Day 5.

Then, you tear apart your books and/or workbooks. Each day's text pages and corresponding worksheet goes into the correct folder. If your child needs graph paper for their math work, that goes in there as well. If you're doing art on Thursdays, you might include the watercolor paper in the Thursday folders. Science labs on Tuesday? Put the lab sheets  in Tuesday's folders. This takes a long time, but when you're finished, your child can simply grab that day's folder and go work. This method is much less stressful on a day-to-day basis and helpful for when you're doing academics in the car or your child is being minded by others. Plus, you're guaranteed not to fall behind without knowing it.

Planners: Paper or Digital?

There are a handful of businesses that offer paper planners specifically for homeschooling parents. Jenn recommends Plum Paper Planners,[2] because their paper is lovely and their binding is sturdy. They also offer a completely customizable layout specifically for homeschooling parents. Many other printed teacher planners are usable but have too many sections that aren't applicable to homeschooling. For those parents who like to plan out their whole school year in advance, a paper planner is a great preview of the work their child will do. The advantage of a paper planner done in pencil is that you can erase and edit as the school year goes on. If you're not a writing fan, you can buy digital daily lesson plans from various curricula providers, print the daily lessons out, and tape them in the correct slots. Yes, we've done this.

There are companies who sell "school-in-a-box" kits with the day-by-day paper planners already created for you. All you have to do is open the planner, turn to the appropriate week and day of school, and go down the checklist. This is one way to ensure rigor in your homeschool.

Courtney prefers electronic planners because they offer more flexibility in changing the schedule as the year goes on. She's had a subscription to Scholaric for several years. One advantage of electronic planners is that you don't have to hand write every assignment for every subject for 180 days of school. Generally, electronic planners will let you input codes that automatically schedule out for the entire year. Most of these planners also allow you to customize your holidays, so that your schedule is automatically created around your family's off time. These auto-schedules can be done at half-speed, or double-time, too. If you have digital lesson plans, you can simply copy and paste those in the correct days. If you want to schedule read-alouds, this is a great place to drop those titles in, as well. If you make use of YouTube videos or other websites, you can also place those links where they need to be for your child. Finally, some electronic planners come pre-loaded with popular homeschool curricula, which makes your life easier.

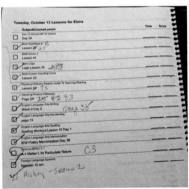

If you find yourself working ahead, you can "bump back" days, and if you're behind, you can "bump forward" days, so that you can easily see how much

2   plumpaper.com/shop/category/homeschool-teacher

longer you have in the school year. For those who live in higher regulation states or who have high school students, electronic planners can also keep track of the number of minutes your child has studied and automatically create printable report cards and transcripts. Most electronic planners also allow you to create a child account, so that as your child goes through their day they can log in and check off their work and click the links for videos or websites. Courtney still likes paper, though, so she prints these daily schedules out and binds them.

How Long Does It Take?

Teaching your child at home will take less time than they'd spend at public school, but more time than helping them with their homework. A general rule of thumb is a minimum of 15 minutes per year of age of seatwork, per day. This rule works out to a 5-year-old kindergartner spending about 75 minutes a day (an hour and 15 minutes) on academics, a 10-year-old fourth grader spending about 150 minutes per day (two and a half hours), and a 15-year-old ninth grader spending 225 minutes per day (three and three-quarters of an hour) with their butt in a seat, learning. This does not include bedtime reading, independent reading, nature walks, physical exercise, music lessons, and so on. Any time off task will only add to that total, so if you take breaks (and of course you do!) then the total homeschool day will be longer than those numbers.

Number of recommended seated, on-task instructional minutes, by age.

age 5	75 minutes
age 6	90 minutes
age 7	105 minutes
age 8	120 minutes
age 9	135 minutes
age 10	150 minutes
age 11	165 minutes
age 12	180 minutes
age 13	195 minutes
age 14	210 minutes
age 15	225 minutes

age 16	240 minutes
age 17	255 minutes
age 18	270 minutes

Stereotypes about learning abound, and one of those is that young boys or active young girls simply aren't capable of sitting still long enough to learn to read or do other academics at early ages. While we'll be the first to admit that young children are wiggly and need frequent rest breaks, we also think that they're capable of sitting down and learning. Yes, even those children with autism, ADHD, and other health issues. By helping your young children with a gradual increase in expectations, daily aerobic exercise, and a warm, supportive home atmosphere, your young child can learn and thrive while doing academics.

CHAPTER 4

CHOOSING QUALITY CURRICULA

We believe this topic is so important that we're giving it its own chapter plus an appendix. After setting your educational goals, choosing high-quality curricula is the most important step you can take toward providing your child with an excellent education at home.

It Used to Be So Easy...

When Jenn started homeschooling, she didn't know any secular homeschoolers, so she assumed she was going to have to use religious materials. For the first two years, she used Seton, a "school at home" Catholic provider. They made it easy to get started, with workbooks and daily lesson plans. Jenn mailed in tests to be graded by a "real" teacher. Abeka and Bob Jones are similar "school at home" providers except geared toward the evangelical market instead of the Catholic one served by Seton. Drew mostly followed the recommendations in *The Well-Trained Mind* by Susan Wise Bauer and Jessie Wise, with some additions from Ambleside Online, a traditional Charlotte Mason program. At one point, to simplify reporting to the local district, they also used Kolbe Academy, a Catholic classical provider. Today, just scrolling through Instagram for five minutes will turn up more curriculum options than we had all told in the early '00s. How do you choose?

Guidelines for Evaluating Curriculum

Evaluating curriculum is both harder and easier than it seems. It's harder because there's just so much of it out there! You don't know what to look for. You don't know how to eliminate the duds. How are you supposed to choose?

Once you do know what your goals are, and what science tells us are reliable ways to get there, eliminating huge swathes of curriculum becomes surprisingly easy. This often narrows your choices down to only a few options.

Expertise Matters

When we evaluate a curriculum, we start by looking for three basic things:

1. The author should have substantial subject matter expertise.
2. The program should have undergone field-testing.
3. The program should have been written for use with average students, not just gifted ones.

All three of these points can be boiled down to one thing: professionalism. Don't waste your money on curriculum that doesn't meet basic quality standards.

Subject Expertise

We don't want to dump on enterprising homeschool parents with graphic design skills and a social media presence, but just because someone made pretty math worksheets for their kids and decided to sell them on Instagram or Teachers Pay Teachers does not mean you want to use those worksheets with *your* kids. Unless the author also holds degrees in mathematics and education, it's likely that those worksheets will be, if not exactly harmful, at least a waste of your money and your children's time.

How do you know if the author of a curriculum has expertise? One easy thing you can do is look at their author biography. Check their educational background, work experience, and previous academic publications. You want to see relevant background that points toward graduate-level knowledge of the subject. That's the ideal. There are exceptions, of course, but these criteria act as a baseline to determine whether a person actually has the expertise to be creating a curriculum.

Veteran homeschoolers can also have a lot to offer, whether or not they have university degrees. We know many homeschooling parents who are effectively independent scholars, sometimes with decades of teaching experience. Becoming a homeschooler is joining a community, and we can support our community by patronizing these small curriculum providers, online teachers, private tutors, and curriculum consultants.

Field-Testing

Another key item to look for is whether the curriculum has been field-tested in the environment(s) for which it was intended. For example, back in 2011, Drew published an elementary language curriculum called *I Speak Latin*. Drew's doctorate is in Germanic Languages and Literatures, not Classics, although their area of specialization—medieval literature—required them to learn Latin in graduate school. Their degree also included multiple classes in language pedagogy. Beginning in 2008, Drew mined all these facets of their academic background to develop *I Speak Latin*, but they also field-tested it over a period of four years with homeschooling families, in a cottage school, and in a private school. We like curricula that have been tested like this to get all the bugs out.

Average Is Not a Dirty Word

We also want to see programs that are not designed exclusively for use with academically gifted students.

Don't get us wrong. We love gifted students, and each of us has at least one child with academic gifts. However, programs written for gifted students (often by gifted adults) may rely on less-than-optimal teaching methods because the author assumes that gifted kids are able to fill in the missing pieces themselves. That may be true...or it may not. The academically gifted and autistic child may not, in fact, infer details about social interactions or motivations that are left unstated. Likewise, a neurotypical child who is lacking specific background knowledge on a given topic may not be able to make sense of an assignment that relies on that knowledge. And few children will do well with a curriculum that assumes skills in the subjects the child may not have; gifted students are often asynchronous learners, with uneven development across academic domains.

That's why we will almost always go for a curriculum that the average or below-average student can use successfully. (Bonus: Your gifted child can still use it at an accelerated pace.) Curricula like these will require harder work on your part and on the student's part—and more effort means better learning outcomes.[1]

Committing information to long-term memory is hard work. This process isn't always going to make your kid happy, and it may come packaged in a form that looks excruciatingly boring to you. Courtney will confess that she almost fell asleep doing phonics exercises with her youngest, but her daughter needed the practice, so she persevered. One night she and her daughter co-read a Spanish-English picture book called *Señorita Mariposa* (Ben Gundersheimer, 2019), and it was a beautiful sight to watch her daughter sound out the English word "admire" and then recognize the Spanish cognate. All those phonics drills didn't kill her daughter's love of learning. Instead, it opened her up not only to her native language, but to a new one as well.

---

1   Bjork, E and Bjork R A (2011) "Making Things Hard on Yourself, But in a Good Way: Creating Desirable Difficulties to Enhance Learning". In M A Gernsbacher, R W Pew, L M Hough, J R Pomerantz (Eds.) & FABBS Foundation, *Psychology and the real world: Essays illustrating fundamental contributions to society* (pp. 56–64). Worth Publishers.

Additional Signs that a Curriculum Was Developed by Experts

A good curriculum will come with a *pacing guide*, which shows the approximate rate at which average students can move through the material. If you're using materials created for classrooms, you'll probably need to adjust the pacing. Often, although not always, you'll be able to move through the material more quickly. As a homeschooler, you can and should adapt your pacing to the needs of your children. At the same time, you can use the pacing guide to help keep you on track as you move through the school year. If you find yourself regularly falling behind for reasons other than unusual learning needs, it's time to refocus and pick up the pace. Some excellent curricula do not have an explicit pacing guide; the time frame is dictated by the number of lessons and the number of days in the school year (180 is typical in the United States).

A good curriculum will also come with questions that have *sample answers*. It's easy to create a question, but it's much more difficult to create a set of realistic answers. You need to know what a typical grade level answer to that specific question looks like, so that you can help your student reach that standard. Content standards and objectives sometimes have proficiency guides for various standards, but that doesn't help you on page 17 of *Frankenstein*.

A good curriculum will also have *prompts or teaching notes* for you, the instructor. "Don't forget to mention the theme of _____ on page 26. Note the literary allusion _____ on pg. 27." Or, prompts might look like an already-created problem set with 80/20 old/new questions, with interleaved, interval-spaced, varied question sets, complete with tips about common errors to warn students against. This sort of thing is like having a mentor in the text. Don't we all need someone who's got your back when the baby was up at 3 am and you discover you're out of coffee?

Finally, a good curriculum will have regular *assessments* that are professionally designed ("psychometrician" is a real job title), and useful to both you and the student. Remember, *formative assessment* forms your teaching, and *summative assessment* sums up what your student has learned. You need both for good teaching. Assessments are distinct from learning activities, such as drills, rehearsals, or other exercises. For more on assessments, see chapter 17.

Cheap, Good, Fast: Pick Two

As experienced home educators know, you can have cheap curricula, good curricula, or fast curricula. Pick any two.

The only wrong answer here is "fast and cheap," with a few rare exceptions that we'll discuss later. "Good and fast" is frequently possible, as is "cheap and good." We understand that most people's homeschool budgets are limited, so it helps to know that a high-quality, scripted curriculum like *The Ordinary Parent's Guide to Teaching Reading* (Jessie Wise and Sara Buffington, 2004) costs significantly less than boxed phonics packages like *Hooked on Phonics* or many of the printable reading programs you'll find on Instagram.

More Things to Look For

Here are some guidelines we've developed over the years for evaluating curriculum. We think they'll serve you as well as they've served us.

- **Avoid FOMO.** Make sure that your materials fit your long-term plan. To borrow a phrase from Clinton Kelly and Stacy London in *What Not to Wear,* buy ~~clothes~~ curriculum for the plan and children you have, not the plan and children you want. While it may be tempting to snatch up that unit study on the history of the potato chip, make sure that the bulk of your curriculum supports your children's long-term academic growth.

- **Is it better than what you're currently using?** Our curmudgeonly tendencies apply to the new hot (and often totally unproven) thing, too. New does not necessarily mean improved. How does that curriculum compare in a head-to-head competition against what you're currently using? Or against the tried-and-true offering that has served homeschoolers well for decades? Why would you change what you're using if the new thing isn't better? When someone asks about a math program, we'll compare it to existing homeschool curricula. That's a long list and it'd have to be something special for us to say, "Oh, that's definitely better; you should use it."

- **Scripts are your friend.** If there is a scripted option, pick that one. Scripted curriculum is a support, not a prison. You don't have to use the script, but on days when there isn't enough coffee in the entire world to tame your brain weasels, the script is your friend. If the curriculum doesn't have a script, make sure that it at least includes summaries, questions and their answers, and notes for you.

- **Can you open and go?** Maybe you have time and mental energy to shuffle across multiple books to create a daily list of activities, but many parents don't. Busy homeschooling parents have limited time and executive function, and they need something that they can count on to tell them what to do and when, or the subject often won't get taught.

- **Questions should have answers.** Look at samples. Almost all curriculum will have samples on their webpage, and if the one you're looking at doesn't, that should give you pause. Make sure that, in the question and answer segment, it doesn't just say, "Answers may vary." Even when it is actually true that the answer *will* vary, as is often the case with short-answer or essay questions, you at least want some possible examples there. "Answers will vary" is a clue that the instructional designer didn't "dog food" the curriculum—it hasn't been used with real children. You also want some indication that the program has been beta-tested on children who are not the author's own family.

- **The perfect is the enemy of the good.** Another question to ask is, "What are the strengths and weaknesses of this program?" There is no One, True, Perfect curriculum. Everything has good and bad points, and we need to be honest about what those are in order to make a useful evaluation. For example, Fishtank English Language Arts does a good job with inclusive choices of literature, but it is lacking in explicit instruction in composition. That might be fine with you if you're using a dedicated composition program alongside it, but you'll want to be aware that it will require that kind of supplementation before you buy it.

- **Don't judge a book by its cover.** Good graphic design does not ensure that a curriculum is pedagogically sound. Of course, you want something that's legible and well organized—and fine, maybe you just hate poor old Comic Sans. However, just because it looks pretty doesn't mean it's going to do the job for your family. You want a good match between the author's educational philosophy and your own, which means that both the author and you need to know what those philosophies are and have clearly articulated them.

- **What about prerequisites?** Beast Academy, a math curriculum for gifted children, doesn't start in kindergarten, although they're working their way down. What do children need to know before they start there? Killgallon's writing program is great for refining sentence-level composition, but students need some solid skills in comprehension and text generation before they start with it. Do you really want to start your child's history education with American history? How do you explain colonists without explaining Native Americans first? Or King George without explaining Great Britain first? Prerequisites matter.

- **Where is the scope and sequence?** If a curriculum doesn't offer a scope and sequence—a document that explains what is covered in the curriculum and in what order—then you might want to stop and think twice, because the author probably hasn't. Your homeschool planning depends on someone else's curricular planning, and if you can't count on that, the whole building rests on a weak foundation.

- **Does it have actual lessons?** We have forgotten the number of times someone has excitedly told us about a curriculum—often a pricey curriculum—with no lessons. A list of possible handcrafts and YouTube videos is not a lesson. Good lessons include a materials list; retrieval practice; a prerequisite knowledge check; step-by-step presentation of new information in small chunks; built-in checks for understanding with specific examples and nonexamples and common mistakes; diagrams of concepts; guided practices and scaffolds for independent practice with, preferably, 20% new problems and 80% old problems, not to mention formative and summative assessments. We also need to know how the product interlocks with other curricula. None of that? None of our money.

- **Is it usable for neurodivergent households?** This question doesn't apply to everyone, but it's a good quality marker. Those of us with neurodivergent households—with family members who are autistic or ADHD or learning disabled or different in some way from the "standard" human—want curricula that work for us, too. Does a given curriculum lean on interpreting social situations without much explicit instruction? Probably not a good fit. Does it require shuffling around three or four different texts every day in order to teach it? Not easily usable for us. Does it require lots of hand-copying of material? Either we're going to alter the way we use it, or we're not going to use it at all. Is there little review and practice for the student who needs lots of extra reinforcement? Hard pass. We don't have the luxury of using so-so curricula and getting away with it, because we'll end up with children who aren't learning.

Other signs of a good curriculum include:

- prerequisite knowledge checks
- deliberate linking to prior knowledge
- lesson outlines that detail instructions and assignments
- simple, clear, concrete instructions
- examples *and* non-examples
- *useful* pictures and graphs, not distracting
- interleaved, interval-spaced, varied practice
- 80/20 old information/new problem practice split
- *detailed* rubrics for successful assignments, not above/middle/below
- long assignments broken into smaller chunks
- frequent (at least weekly) quizzes
- time expectations for assignments
- extra practice for that difficult concept
- low distraction black and white

Things to Avoid

We've given you lots of ideas about what to look for in a curriculum along with some red flags. What else should you avoid when choosing curriculum?

The Entertainment Trap

We're about to make the kind of statement that causes some homeschoolers to roll their eyes. We're going to say it anyway.

Learning is not always fun and trying to entertain your kids 24/7 will not result in more or better learning.

The popular education blog Cult of Pedagogy has a great article and podcast related to this, called "Is Your Lesson a Grecian Urn?"[2] We encourage you to read the article to fully appreciate the reference, but in short, the article asks, Do your homeschool activities have a clearly defined, rigorous academic purpose, or are they just entertaining distractions? Parents need to identify exactly what children are most likely to focus on during a lesson. Those whiz-bang activities from that pretty Instagram curriculum may actually turn out to be distractions, pulling your child's attention away from the things you want them to be thinking about.

---

2   Gonzalez, J (2016) "Is Your Lesson a Grecian Urn?", bit.ly/3euH8cs

Remember, as Daniel Willingham, a well-respected cognitive scientist, says, "We learn what we think about."

In his 2009 book *Why Don't Students Like School?*, Willingham argues, "a teacher's goal should almost always be to get students to think about *meaning*" (pg. 66). The trick is that meaning varies in context. A good curriculum will establish that context for your students with background knowledge checks. For example, "Tammy, remember when we went to the aviary? What makes a bird, a bird?"

How do you get your child to think about meaning? Well, it's not just interest— we've all picked up a book we were sure we were going to love, but found it dreadfully boring, despite our burning interest in the subject. This is often true for our children with classic literature, but a good curriculum will explain the context enough to bring those books to life for your children. So does the entertainment factor matter? Not exactly. Simply doing a dramatic read-aloud of a beloved classic is not going to get the job done. What works is, as Willingham says is "[t]he emotional bond between students and teacher..." (pg. 70).

This is why we say that homeschooling is parenting first. You have to have a good emotional bond for effective homeschooling. But while good relationships are necessary, they are also insufficient on their own. Willingham goes on to say, "...the funny teacher, or the gentle storytelling teacher, whose lessons are poorly organized won't be much good either. Effective teachers have both qualities. They are able to connect personally with students, and they organize the material in a way that makes it interesting and easy to understand" (pg. 70). This is where a good curriculum is critical—it will organize the material for you, so you can concentrate on connecting with your children.

A Word About All-in-One Workbooks

One of the many educational hats Courtney wears is "homeschool portfolio assessor." Every year she reviews dozens of homeschool portfolios, and during the time she's been doing this work, she's evaluated the work of hundreds of homeschooled children in West Virginia. And every year, she is shocked by how many work samples are drawn exclusively from those "complete curriculum" workbooks you can pick up at your local big box store or Barnes & Noble.

"Everything you need to know" workbooks are a lie. They are not curricula, nor do they provide anything close to an adequate education. A curriculum teaches new material; a workbook reviews material that's already been learned. Reviews don't need to be as lengthy or complete as a full curriculum because they're just retrieving key bits of material that has already been taught. If you assign those all-in-one books to your child as a wholesale substitute for a curriculum that methodically introduces new material and has your child practice that material to fluency, you are doing your child a great disservice. Even if they do learn something, they will not learn to the standard that they could have achieved with a proper curriculum.

High-quality, affordable homeschool curricula exist, and you should track them down. Don't rely on cheap review books to educate your children. At best, you can use them to keep skills fresh over the summer or to provide extra practice to shore up a child's skills.

School-in-a-Box?

Remember that school-in-a-box program from Seton that Jenn used when she first started homeschooling? While Courtney frequently recommends all-in-one curriculum packages for parents who have decision fatigue, we must acknowledge that there are issues with them. The problems with boxed curricula include:

- **One size fits all.** You probably aren't homeschooling the mythical child that is on the same grade level for every single subject.
- **Expensive.** When you buy a school-in-a-box package, you are buying everything new. Homeschoolers tend to buy a lot of used books because they're cheaper. A curriculum in a box doesn't let you save money.
- **Environmentally unfriendly.** "Reuse, reduce, recycle" or "use it up, make it do, or do without"? Not if you're buying a brand-new box of curriculum and manipulatives every year.
- **Poor pedagogy.** Many school-in-a-box curricula packages are literature-based programs. While we love books, literature-based programs rarely include sufficient vocabulary study, content-specific retrieval practice, systematic and thorough composition skill building, grammar study and text-specific grammar analysis, or summative testing.
- **Parental effort.** One of the joys of homeschooling is the ability to be flexible, to tweak a curriculum to your child's specific needs. When you get a box filled with a year's worth of curriculum that covers all the subjects, you'll probably want to start tweaking every item to meet your child's specific needs. If you're going to go to all that effort anyway, why not just choose individual curricula that work for your child?

In Praise of Scripted Curricula

We know parents need support. Freestyling might be the mode of choice for musicians or actors with 10,000 hours of practice behind them, but newly homeschooling parents are rarely that skilled. A scripted curriculum strikes a great balance between complete anarchy and drill and kill.

A high-quality scripted curriculum will have key words and ideas highlighted for your child to focus on. It will provide a short review or link to a previous lesson before new material is introduced. You can switch up how the answers are given, allowing your child to circle the correct answer instead of re-writing, for example. Working one-on-one, it's also easy to have your child say the answers out loud instead of writing them. With a high-quality scripted curriculum, you will almost always find a rubric or other descriptor of a correct answer.

Organizers and pacing guides are almost always included in a high-quality curriculum, allowing you to easily create daily to-do lists. Often, an assignment notebook in the form of daily lesson plans is provided. When that happens, the big projects are already broken down into smaller pieces, with shorter deadlines. If you bought a curriculum printed in color, judicious use of highlighting is often already done for you.

Homeschooling parents don't *need* to create their own materials. Can you? Sure. Is it fun to create a craft or other activity for your child? Sometimes! But, on a day-to-day basis, most people need some kind of help. Life comes at you fast, and you need to be able to just open the book and walk your child through a lesson in 30 minutes or less, because you have other things to do that day.

Fortunately, experts have created high-quality, scripted curricula for you to use, in every subject, every day. Even when you're fully caffeinated, scripted curricula are faster and easier to teach when you're in it for the long haul. You don't need to guess whether you've done enough for the day. If you finished the lesson, that's it! Move on to the next subject.

If you have a long-term plan, you can adjust for factors like a newly released curriculum, or the realization that what you used for your oldest kid may not work as well for younger siblings.

Money Matters

Scripted curricula are usually comparatively cheap. For example, a second grade year centered on scripted curricula (though not entirely composed of it) and pieced together second hand from ThriftBooks and new from Rainbow Resources, along with judicious use of a library card, could be done for less than $150. (Yes, we priced out a rigorous, research-informed, full-year curriculum that covers all the core subjects on grade level for less than a monthly electricity bill.) Much of this can be resold to help finance next year's curriculum.

In comparison, a popular curriculum package for new users is $600 at the time of this writing.

One advantage of the curriculum package is that it has a beautiful manual. Day by day, you open the manual, and it tells you exactly what to do.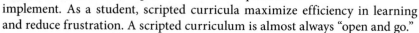

Scripted curricula are fast for both you and your child. As the teacher, scripted curricula are quick to implement. As a student, scripted curricula maximize efficiency in learning and reduce frustration. A scripted curriculum is almost always "open and go."

The Children We Have

The curricula you choose must work for the children you actually have, not the perfect angels in the stock photo on the publisher's website. For example, some kids absolutely love workbooks, and others find them dull as dirt. Similarly, if you have a kid with dyspraxia, choosing a program that requires a lot of writing by hand (again, those workbooks!) will mean that you need to find accommodations, like speech-to-text apps or scribing. If you choose a literature-heavy curriculum for a child with dyslexia, then you'll need to track down audiobooks for all those texts or commit to reading them all aloud to your child. If you have a child with ADHD and you choose a video-based curriculum, they may be unable to attend to the videos and need text-based alternatives instead.

We've made these mistakes ourselves. Courtney spent months reading up on math curricula before she started working with her eldest child, and she eventually settled on Singapore math. They did three years of it, and then Courtney realized that her daughter was retaining almost nothing in terms of math facts, despite Courtney's diligence  in adhering to the home instructor's guide and her child's work in the extra practice books. Courtney still loves Singapore math, but for a child with a math learning disability like her daughter, it just did not work. Courtney had to switch to Saxon, which she had previously regarded with horror. To make it up, Courtney's daughter spent fourth grade doing double math, from 1 to 4 every afternoon. She'd cry and then Courtney would cry and then she'd cry again. But now she's working on grade level and even a bit ahead because Courtney was willing to be flexible in terms of curriculum.

Considerations for Outsourcing

There are probably subjects that you can't or simply don't want to teach, no matter how good the curriculum. Don't be afraid to outsource these subjects to experts. Hiring tutors, signing your child up for classes, and going hard on free club projects are all good ways to make sure your child gains the knowledge you've decided that they need. By wisely choosing tutors, Courtney has outsourced everything from Latin to literature with good results. Like many homeschoolers, Jenn is a fan of community college during high school, particularly for sciences with labs. In 4th grade, Drew's daughter earned a sash full of Girl Scout badges, rounding out her academic program with a wide range of arts, STEM, and life skills topics. Keep in mind that as the homeschooling parent, you're still the educator-in-charge, which means you ensure the work gets done.

When outsourcing, there are so many options that you may feel a bit like a child in a candy store, but pick and choose carefully. What happens if you don't have a plan before you begin this process? As Drew says, it's like going to the supermarket hungry and without a shopping list. You're going to come home with $100 worth of junk food, but you still have nothing for dinner. If you don't trust your own decisions because you don't really understand how teaching works and how children learn, you're going to wake up one morning and realize that your third grader is on Zoom all day, every day, and you have no idea if they're learning anything.

We see this all the time. Most discussions boil down to the same issue: parents are over-reliant on an outside authority. In other words, someone who is not you, the homeschooling parent, becomes the architect of your child's education. If you're clear about your goals, and you know what the science says about what works in education, you won't end up giving your children the educational equivalent of Doritos for dinner. And you won't feel like you have to order takeout every night of the week, either.

Courtney has been teaching online for a couple of decades, and she has thoughts about when and how to search for a good course. First, accreditation is surprisingly useless. Generally speaking, accreditation is more like getting married than getting a driver's license. Essentially, all an educational institution has to do is show up with the right paperwork and the right amount of money. The accreditation organization checks the paperwork, asks a few questions of the individuals in charge to make sure they're on the up and up, and boom! Accreditation issued. Unlike a driver's license, no special skills are required to be demonstrated. Therefore, looking for an accredited school is not as important as you'd think.

When looking for a class, make sure you know what you want in advance. For example, if your high school student wants to take art as a credit and you don't feel qualified to instruct high school level art, then go seek out an art class designed for high school students as a high school credit. While art lessons are good, and can be used as a spine for your child's high school art class, weekly hour-long lessons alone aren't enough for a full subject's credit. This holds true for swimming lessons, piano lessons, and so on. The standard Carnegie unit, used to determine credit, is defined as *120 hours of contact time with an instructor*—i.e., one hour of instruction a day, five days a week, for 24 weeks, or 7,200 minutes of instructional time over the course of an academic year. Also, keep in mind that a class for any age should have daily assignments so that students master and retain the information taught during class sessions.

Typically, we recommend a class offered by a reputable organization, one with several years of well-regarded operations. Ask around in your support system for recommendations. While there are many individual tutors, hiring one can go sideways quickly. At one point, Courtney shelled out several hundred dollars in advance, and then the tutor disappeared for a month in the spring. If you do hire a tutor, make sure that they have experience in your child's age group. Someone accustomed to working with college students is going to have a rough time tutoring a 6-year-old. We recommend asking for references and checking those references.

If your child has an issue with a class at an online organization, you want some kind of human administration that you can appeal to, either for a refund or a substitute teacher. There should be a phone number, not just an email address. The administration should provide an academic calendar, grading policies, late policies, and attendance policies in writing, in advance. If there are billing issues, you want to be able  to take that up with the payments division, instead of trying to negotiate with someone who is grading your child's work. The administration should handle the contracts, not the teacher.

Whether online or face to face, when searching for a course, you want a full-fledged syllabus that describes in detail what will be covered, when it will be covered throughout the year, and what the policies are for turning in work. When reading the syllabus and course description, the education method should be easy to understand. A good syllabus is at least two pages, minimum, and often runs to five or seven pages. If you're signing up for a course through an organization, they should have a family handbook with a behavior policy, philosophy of education, and parent and child expectations for participation.

Some questions are easier to find answers for. Will the instructor perform live demonstrations? This matters for your child, because not all children will easily learn from simply watching other people work. Are the students expected to form small groups and discuss the content on their own? Small group discussion is extraordinarily difficult to do well, and unless the teacher is skilled at teaching students how to productively discuss the material, that format rarely yields much learning. Students end up talking about their favorite video games or music videos, instead, which is great for socialization but not so great for learning. If the class is online, will your child be expected to scan handwritten work and turn that in? If you don't own a scanner or have poor Internet access, a policy like that can quickly make the class unworkable for your child.

What kind of homework will be assigned? If there is insufficient practice of the knowledge, skills, and abilities being taught, your child is unlikely to retain anything. Discussion forums alone don't cut it. A class that meets only once a week or every other week might expect your child to do too much by themselves. Information is best learned in frequent, small bites, not a firehose of information once a week. Will your child be expected to do research projects more or less by themselves? Adults spend years learning how to do research for PhDs, so be suspicious of classes that blithely expect children to do research for essays, projects, and so on without spending a good chunk of the class teaching children how to do research.

Is information provided in multiple formats? For best retention, the teacher should speak the information, your child should read the information, and your child should write about the information. Ideally, your child will be engaged in conversation throughout the class, whether they like it or not. In some classes, they should also be practicing the information, whether in labs or by creating final products. The more opportunities your child has to work with the material, the better they will learn it.

These are not the only concerns, but they are some of the more common questions you want to have answered when you decide to outsource a class. For many homeschooling families, outsourcing is a valuable part of their homeschool, especially as children get older. Upper level math, science, literature, and history are all complex subjects that many families feel are best taught by subject matter experts. Luckily, the homeschool community has many fine offerings available.

CHAPTER 5
CREATING AND IMPLEMENTING A TEACHING PLAN

By now, you know that we strongly prefer to use high-quality scripted curricula written by subject experts, and we've explained some of our reasons for that preference. In this chapter, we're going to show you another reason: Planning out a curriculum from scratch is not for the faint of heart. If you choose a high-quality curriculum with actual lessons, all you need to do is figure out how many lessons there are and how many school days you have to teach them, then slot them into your planning calendar. If you don't, well…read on to see the process that those subject experts use to create the kinds of curriculum we recommend. Along the way, we'll give you a brief history of the standards movement and suggest some ways to think about standards as a homeschooler.

Content Standards and Objectives

Once you've determined your philosophy of education, then you can decide on your content standards and objectives (CSOs). Public school teachers are usually required to teach CSOs provided by their state, and you can often find these on your state's department of education website.

Standards are the knowledge, skills, and abilities that children should possess at different ages and stages. As a parent, we're already familiar with a good many of these; for example, we know that children should start walking between nine and fifteen months, or that they should have 50 words by age two. The problem comes when we begin to distinguish between what psychologist David Geary calls *biologically primary knowledge*—or things that children just pick up from typical surroundings, like walking and talking—and *cultural artifacts*, like reading, math, and history. Because the latter are not innate, but rather, artificial constructs of our current human culture, we must deliberately and specifically teach these to children. For example, apart from a few hyperlexic and/or profoundly gifted children who crack the phonetic code on their own, most children require systematic instruction in phonics in order to learn to read.

Academic standards come into play when we say children should learn to read *this* well at *that* grade level.

Do we need CSOs? Absolutely. Is a good CSO set complex and difficult to understand? Mm-hmm. Is it excruciatingly specific, with detailed levels of complexity and exemplars at each grade level? Yes. Does it reference how the concepts progress within each standard and grade? Across grades? It should.

CSOs help you answer questions like: What should your 18-year-old know, as a legal adult? What's the minimum? The maximum? What of that can or should be taught with formal academics? Taught in the school setting? How must these skills be developed over time? What would that look like at 16? 12 years old? 8 years old? 4 years old? How do you build and reinforce the knowledge, skills, and abilities within and across disciplines? Good content standards and objectives are a bit like DNA's double helix: spiraling from year to year, revisiting the same themes and content, going more in-depth each year, held together by links across subjects.

A Short History Lesson: Where Did the Common Core Standards Come From?

Courtney thinks it behooves us to step back and review a little history here. The three of us are old enough to remember the Cold War, although we're a little too young to remember the Space Race. The US government was afraid that the Soviets were going to beat us to space, so it encouraged schools to train more scientists, especially engineers. This renewed national emphasis on our education system led to statements like the *A Nation at Risk* report in 1983. Here's a quote from that report: "If an unfriendly foreign power had attempted to impose on America the mediocre educational performance that exists today, we might well have viewed it as an act of war."

As the nation geared up to do educational battle on the world stage in the late 1980s and early 1990s, the US Department of Education quite sensibly decided that we would need to know when we won, and awarded grants to various professional organizations to determine national standards in all subjects. To quote education researcher Diane Ravitch (2010) in *The Death and Life of the Great American School System*, "We thought that if the standards were written by teachers and scholars in every field, if they reflected the wisdom of teachers, if they were faithful to the field, states and districts would find them worthy of adoption, in whole or in part."

However, in 1994, Lynne V. Cheney, fresh from her post as chairperson of the National Endowments for the Humanities (which had partially funded these tentative national standards!) attacked the history standards, written at UCLA, for political bias. It became a huge cause *célèbre*, turning the idea of federally sponsored national standards into a political third rail that no politician wanted to touch.

However, the sense of national urgency about the quality of our educational system had not abated, and it was in this climate that the *No Child Left Behind* (NCLB) act was passed. Because standards themselves were taboo, the law focused not on content, but on test results—and only in math and English language arts. (No politics here, no siree!) Except now, NCLB needed a national set of standards to decide what to test on, and so at the height of the federal privatization movement, the feds reached out to lesser-known organizations, specifically "the National Governors Association, the Council of Chief State School Officers, a business-sponsored group called Achieve, and a group led by David Coleman called Student Achievement Partners" (*The Death and Life of the Great American School System*, Ravitch, 2010). David Coleman, by the way, was president of the College Board, which owns the SAT—hardly a neutral party. Then, the feds refused to give states a significant portion of federal funding (which is typically 8% of school funding, a big chunk of change) unless they adopted these privately written standards in English language arts and math, which are now known as the Common Core standards. Although adoption was technically voluntary, these financial incentives forced many states to adopt the Common Core.

Public School Standards

Here in the United States, states have content standards and objectives that are to be taught at each grade level. In most cases, those state standards are based on the national standards developed by national organizations, like the National Council for the Social Studies. Sometimes the standards were supported by philanthropic organizations like the Carnegie Corporation of New York, which funded the development of the *Next Generation Science Standards*. Other subjects also have national standards. For example, there are *National Core Arts Standards* and *World-Readiness Standards for Learning Languages*. Keep in mind that all of these national standards are not mandatory, and states can choose to adopt them or not.

It's important to remember that, prior to this era of standards, many teachers taught more or less whatever they felt like. Courtney remembers her father designing his public school science classes in the early 1980s. The assumption that all students have to meet the same academic standards is a relatively new idea. There were some exceptions, like the New York Regents exams, but historically, teachers had much more professional latitude than they do today. Private schools tend to retain a significant part of this educational independence—in West Virginia, private schools do not have to be accredited or teach the state standards. Of course, homeschoolers everywhere still have that freedom.

Why Do We Care about Public School Standards?

Aren't standards only a public school issue? Can't homeschoolers just ignore them? Yes and no. There are a couple of reasons you might want to keep one eye on your state or provincial standards.

One is that you might not keep homeschooling very long. In fact,

> Isenberg found that only 48% of homeschooled children from religious homes and only 15% of those from secular homes continue to homeschool for more than six years; homeschooling grows less common as children age, even among highly educated, more affluent families.[1]

Therefore, you might want to make sure that your children don't have any gaps when they slide back into public schools because chances are, they will. (Jenn's and Courtney's families are in that 15%, by the way, while Drew's daughter graduated from a public charter school.)

In addition, we can't always automatically assume that homeschooling beats public schooling every time. There are some excellent public schools out there. Courtney knows this first-hand because she lives in one of the best districts in her state. There is not much peer-matched research on homeschooling, but what there is states that "homeschooling does not have much of an effect at all on student achievement once family background variables are controlled for" (Kunzman and Gaither, 2013, 18). There are a couple of smaller studies that make the point that structured homeschooling does give an advantage, but more research is required to definitively say that's true.

In the end, you want to do at least as well as your child would do in local public schools, and how can you do that if you don't know what they're doing?

We're not going to say that you 100% must do homeschooling a certain way, because we've seen some pretty awesome homeschoolers completely ignore academic standards and their kids turned out just fine. However, when that happens, it's almost always because the child in question is either moderately

---

1   *Homeschooling: A Comprehensive Survey of the Research* by Robert Kunzman & Milton Gaither, 2013, 16.

or profoundly gifted and absorbs information like a dry sponge, and the parent excels at parceling out information to their child. In other words, you're looking at a gifted child or a gifted teacher or both.

For all the rest of us, especially for homeschoolers who have children with one or more learning disabilities or neurodiversities, we really should at least check every now and then and make sure that we're on the same planet as other people. In addition, while we like to think we're at least moderately skilled as teachers, standards have often been written by large groups of subject matter experts and then refined over time. Who are we to say that all of their combined judgment and wisdom doesn't matter to our child? We're going to at least entertain the possibility that they put these things in this order for a reason, and that maybe we should at least consider doing it their way.

Rumsfeld Had a Point

Another thing CSOs offer is a way to minimize the dreaded "educational gaps." Those of you old enough to remember this era in history might recoil in horror, but in 2002, Donald Rumsfeld, who was then President George W. Bush's Secretary of Defense, said:

> As we know, there are known knowns, there are things we know we know. We also know there are known unknowns, that is to say, we know there are some things we do not know. But there are also unknown unknowns, the ones we don't know, we don't know.

When we venture into homeschooling spaces, we see a lot of talk about gaps. The argument runs something like, "We can't possibly teach all the knowledge in the world, so we must teach our children how to learn." We disagree. Children can't learn something if they don't know it exists. Part of our job as home educators is to give our children *known knowns*. The multiplication table is one example. Children should know it exists, *and* they should know it backward and forward.

Our children should also learn about *known unknowns*, calculus, or James Joyce. Not everyone is going to take AP Calculus or read Joyce's *Ulysses*, but students should know that these things exist. Teaching our children intellectual humility—that there are things in the world they know to exist but know little or nothing about—is also a goal for us as home educators. We need to avoid letting them be caught in the Dunning-Kruger effect.[2]

---

2   The Dunning-Kruger effect is a cognitive bias in which people tend to overestimate their own knowledge or abilities.

In order to make this happen we need to systematically lead our children through the various branches of each academic subject. No, they're not going to remember everything forever. And, yes, you're going to leave something out, but at least your child knows that the item exists.

The future is bright—for well-prepared children

We believe that our children should be prepared for adult responsibilities at the end of their homeschool experience, if at all possible. What does this mean?

Almost two-thirds of children will go directly to college. If your child does attend college, that bodes well for their future employment prospects. On average, the unemployment rate for people with college degrees is about half that of people with only a high school diploma.[3] The college wage earnings premium is significant, especially when compared to a high school diploma, but not all college degrees are equal. All of the top ten paying majors are engineering, for example.[4] Nursing and other sciences are also good ways to get a return on your college investment. Music and the arts tend to offer the lowest returns on investment, according to the New America Foundation.

Of non-college students, more than two-thirds began entry-level work, according to the Bureau of Labor Statistics. If you're lucky, entry-level work means that your child will enter into an apprenticeship position for employment as an electrician, carpenter, plumber, commercial driver, pipe fitter, roofer, ironworker, line worker, mason, etc. Over a quarter of people with these kinds of licenses or certificates earn more than the average bachelor's degree recipient, according to the Harvard report, "Pathways to Prosperity."[5] These are good jobs.

How good? According to the Bureau of Labor Statistics, the median annual wage for plumbers, pipefitters, and steamfitters was $59,880 in May 2021, approximately the same as a high school teacher ($61,820), or an anthropologist ($61,910). A high school teacher is generally required to have a bachelor's degree to start[6] (average student loan debt: $36,635) and an anthropologist generally

3   U.S. Bureau of Labor Statistics, "Unemployment rates for persons 25 years and older by educational attainment", bit.ly/3RmyCe4

4   Ostrowski, J (2021) "The most valuable college majors in 2021, ranked", Bankrate, bit.ly/3BeVYfU

5   Symonds, W C, Schwartz, R and Ferguson, R F (2011) "Pathways to prosperity: Meeting the challenge of preparing young Americans for the 21st century", bit.ly/3THgoFD

6   U.S. Bureau of Labor Statistics, "High School Teachers", bit.ly/3TZI6xI

has a master's degree to start (average total student loan debt: $71,287).[7] But an apprentice pipefitter gets paid, often starting at $20 per hour.

On the other hand, approximately two-thirds of people employed in those kinds of physical labor positions are injured on the job.[8] In order to move up to less physical jobs on those career tracks, other skills are required. Being a plumber can bring in $100,000 per year as a small business owner.[9] Bookkeeping and other small business skills are important to ensure that the plumbing business is successful. People skills are important, too. Many electricians and pipefitters work contract to contract and people without good social skills don't get tapped for the new contracts, or less physical jobs.

About one in twenty high school students joins the military. For some young people, this can be a great option. Military service comes with healthcare, housing, retirement benefits, education benefits, and on-the-job training in a variety of careers. Because many people join the military at a relatively young age, they can retire early and start a second career that builds on their time in the military.

Keeping these facts in mind, you can begin to craft a customized plan for your child, one that builds on their strengths, shores up their weaknesses, and eases their path into a career. You cannot get away with only basic education: reading, writing, and arithmetic. In the 21st century, the job market demands more, so you have to teach more.

Scope and Sequence

Finally, we're drilling down into a single subject, or group of closely related subjects (we're looking at you, science and social studies). If you're designing your own curriculum based on CSOs, you need to correlate standards with the actual material you'll be using in your teaching. It's like taking a 3D object and spreading it out into a 2D checklist. That checklist needs to be carefully sequenced, to ensure that prerequisites come first.

---

7   Hanson, M (2021) "Average Graduate Student Loan Debt", Education Data Initiative, bit.ly/3x1sAr4

8   Abdalla, S, Apramian, S S, Cantley, L F and Cullen, M R "Occupation and Risk for Injuries" in C N Mock, R Nugent, O Kobusingye et al (eds) (2017) Injury Prevention and Environmental Health (3rd edition), bit.ly/3erhlBR

9   McDowell, J (2022) "Starting a Plumbing Business? Here's What to Expect", Contractor Magazine, bit.ly/3TPl2Bp

	Term 1	Term 2	Term 3	Term 4
procedure variant 1		•	•	•
procedure variant 2		•	•	•
procedure variant 3			•	•
procedure variant 4	•	•	•	•
procedure variant 5	•	•	•	•
New Concept				
concept variant 1	•	•	•	•
concept variant 2	•	•	•	•
concept variant 3	•	•	•	•
concept variant 4			•	•
concept variant 5			•	•
concept variant 6				•
concept variant 8				•
concept variant 9	•	•	•	•
New Concept				
concept variant 1	•	•	•	•
concept variant 2				•
concept variant 3				•
concept variant 4			•	•
Mastering basic facts	•	•	•	•
Procedure	•	•	•	•
Procedure		•	•	•

Does your curriculum cover a given standard? On what page, or text, or unit, or even semester? When we look for a curriculum, we're going to look for a curriculum that emphasizes declarative and procedural knowledge as well as hands-on work such as labs, outdoor observation, or studio-based art classes. A good curriculum will provide a well-planned scope and sequence of facts and skills to be covered over the course of the year, but the quality of any given scope and sequences varies widely, because even specific content standards are vague.

"Plan and conduct an investigation to describe and classify different kinds of materials by their observable properties."

How much planning is required? What kind of detail is required in the plan? Conduct how, exactly? What kind of documentation is required for the lab? What about lab safety? How do I do this at home?

What qualifies as an "investigation"? Can I just send kids to the park and ask them to come back with different things? Or bring random objects from around the house? How old are the children in this task? How much guidance should I be giving here?

How much detail should be on that description? What keywords are you looking for? Are my children supposed to write in complete sentences? Paragraphs? Maybe I should record a video.

What kind of classification structure (or structures) should I be using? Are we going to talk about the states of matter? How should I describe gasses to my children? If we talk about states of matter, are we going to phase-change the material? Isn't that kind of dangerous?

Are we going to test the materials? If we talk about hardness, are we going to bring up the Mohs scale? Do I need a sink of water for the float or sink test for density?

All this, and we haven't even talked about what an "observable property" is, much less how that works with children who are Deaf or Hard of Hearing, or blind or visually impaired.

What grade level would you assign this standard to? Would you be surprised to learn it's a second-grade standard in the Next Generation Science Standards?

As you can see, a scope and sequence that says we cover that standard in chapter 3, or lesson 27, or with unit 5 is necessary, but again, vagueness works against the quality of the underlying match, which in turn is crucial for good implementation of the standards. A checked box on a list doesn't tell you whether the material considered all these questions and answered them. We have a feeling that major publishers hire this out to grad students in garrets, when the fidelity of the match, checking off concept coverage, is actually vitally important.

Curriculum

Now that our intrepid DIY homeschooler has decided on their philosophy of education, created a set of content standards and objectives, and correlated those with a given set of material via a scope and sequence, they get to actually create the curriculum.

As we've noted, a good curriculum will be written by subject matter experts, ideally with the help of instructional designers. It won't necessarily be designed to meet specific content standards and objectives (that's what the scope and sequence ensures). The inclusion of an instructional designer offers the promise that someone has thought about the proper sequences of material for best learning, designed activities for learning that work with a given age and skill level of students, and created standardized assessments.

A good curriculum will have all of this work as a group in a unit, that is itself set within a thematic sequence, which is then placed within a year, or grade band. Then, in that curriculum, the next year will have picked up on the material that you covered last year, and go back into it, in more depth and with greater expectations for your students.

We think you'll now see why we suggest that the vast majority of homeschooling parents buy and use high-quality, academic curricula rather than taking a DIY approach. Unless you have subject expertise in a major subject area and a background in education and considerable experience with instructional design and the means to field-test your program for several years, it's unlikely you'll be able to produce anything that works as well as even a middle-of-the-road textbook. In addition, choosing curricula that conform to your preferred homeschooling style means that you will minimize pedagogical mismatches. Sticking with a solid curriculum over multiple levels, rather than hopping from one program to another, further helps minimize instructional gaps.

Curriculum Is Not Teaching

You may have noticed that none of this actually talks about how you run your homeschool, or your pedagogy. These are all just tools in your toolbox. In homeschooling, you're the one who gets to decide whether to skip that morning question provided in the curriculum, or whether you want to switch curricula because it doesn't conform with your philosophy of education, or even to use the scope and sequence to switch around units, because you recognize that X isn't really a prerequisite of Y, so the order you teach them in doesn't matter.

We'll offer considerations for teaching each subject in Part II. For now, keep in mind that this is a process. You don't have to get it right the first time around. Your child will not be permanently damaged because you chose a math curriculum that doesn't suit them or a science curriculum without a scope and sequence. The purpose of having a philosophy of education is that it helps you select your own content standards and objectives, which then can lead you to decide what your children are going to study and when (the scope and sequence). After you nail that down, then it's much easier to choose your curricula and teach them.

CHAPTER 6
FINDING SUPPORT

It's time for some real talk. *Homeschooling is hard.* There is no easy answer, no quick fix, and no magical curricular unicorn that will make homeschooling joyous all day, every day. Few homeschoolers stick around past the first couple of years, and the main reason for the high attrition rate is a lack of support. Your life will be better if you seek out a support group that can teach you about the legal requirements in your area, share solid teaching and curriculum advice, and offer social outlets for you and your children.

Build Your Team

Depending on your personality and your preferred method of homeschooling, support groups may come in many different flavors. Here are some common support structures:

- **Co-op**. A co-op is usually a formal weekly meeting of homeschooling families. Typically, a parent will volunteer to teach one or more classes at the co-op. Given clear behavior and academic expectations, a thorough set of safety policies, and a low-cost meeting place, this can be a deep well of support for homeschooling families that lasts for generations, like Courtney's local co-op, Learning Options, Inc.

- **Huddle**. Also known as a pod, a small group of families will pool their resources for one or more family members to either take primary responsibility for teaching the children or hire it out. Often, families will develop close ties as their children socialize and learn together. One caveat is that hiring it out comes with tax and legal responsibilities.

- **Park days**. A well-established homeschool family tradition, this is a loose association of families who get together at a local public park or botanic garden on a weekly basis so that the children can play together. Generally, this appeals to homeschool families with younger children.

- **Classes**. Frequently, local organizations like parks, libraries, or YMCAs will create classes tailored to homeschool children. This can be a great way to meet other like-minded families, particularly if you're comfortable arriving a little early and staying late to chat.

- **Online groups**. Facebook is the major force here, and over the years, both Jenn and Drew have run homeschooling support groups on the platform. Jenn's group, Inclusive Academic Homeschoolers, eventually became so popular that she turned over the reins to other people. No matter what your preferred flavor of homeschooling is, you can find a Facebook group for it. Discussion boards, such as those run by the Well-Trained Mind, can be another fantastic source of support. We should note, however, that online groups can exacerbate FOMO, and that peer support is not a substitute for professional advice. (See chapter 19 for more on this subject.)

Jenn says, "In my case, as a home educator, local groups were a disaster. Online support proved to be invaluable to me as a teacher. The folks at The Well-Trained Mind Press host an online forum that was my lifeline in the early days. You may have no one local that understands academic homeschooling, or secular homeschooling, and interacting even online can be such a boost to your self confidence."

Jenn's daughter found support through the You Media department at the Chicago Public Library. She gathered there weekly all through high school with homeschooled students from all over the city and suburbs. They had everything from recording studios to 3D printers and other crafting equipment all free for the kids to use. Your library may have something similar.

Drew also found local support groups to be a bust. Almost all the home educators they met in their western Massachusetts community were unschoolers who didn't know what to make of a 6-year-old learning Latin. Instead, they found social outlets for their daughter through art classes and Girl Scouts. Drew got most of their homeschooling support from online forums like the one hosted by the Well-Trained Mind. (That's where they met Jenn, in fact!)

While the well-established local co-op was helpful for Courtney's initial worries about socialization and meeting senior homeschoolers in the area, her tight work schedule, emphasis on academic secular homeschooling with a precocious reader, and caregiving duties mean that many face-to-face opportunities are unavailable. Instead, prior to the pandemic, Courtney made her own support system by leading homeschooler Girl Scout troops and 4-H clubs, leaning on friends and family for assistance with transporting her children to the weekly co-op, serving on the state board of the WVHEA, moderating local Facebook groups, and signing her children up for swim team and arts lessons.

PART II

THE SCIENCE OF EDUCATION: FROM THEORY TO PRACTICE

When you decide to homeschool, you're taking on a full-time teaching job in addition to your parenting role and any other work you may do. While we don't believe that you need to have a graduate degree in education to homeschool successfully, you do need to know something about how humans—especially young humans—learn. Thankfully, we have plenty of scientific evidence on this topic. In this section, we'll review that evidence and explain how to apply it to become a better and more effective teacher as you teach the various subjects.

CHAPTER 7
NOTES ON HOW HUMANS LEARN

This chapter is probably the most technical part of this book. We've tried to condense the contents of many books and scientific journal articles into an easily comprehensible format because we believe this information is vital to successful homeschooling. If you don't understand how children learn, you're likely to frustrate them and yourself. Successful educators work *with* human nature, not against it, and we need science to explain the mechanics of working with our weird and wonderful brains.

First, we'll introduce a working definition of "learning" from the point of view of neuroscience. Then we'll take you through some basic terminology to help you understand how the brain processes and stores new information and what you can do to make that process work better. Next, we'll explain how to make that information stick in your child's mind with retrieval practice, including what some homeschoolers call *memory work*. These teaching tools will help you teach the individual subjects—to which we turn in the remaining chapters of this section.

Learning Is Memorization

A few months ago, Courtney was reading a Twitter thread that AP Psychology teacher Blake Harvard had started off by pointing out how little teachers learn about memory in most education school classes. There was some disagreement and then Dylan Wiliam waded in with this tweet:

> Actually, that is the only thing I think we should be teaching for. If students can't recall something we have taught from their memory, then our teaching has been a complete waste of time. (@dylanwiliam 1:39 PM · Apr 4, 2022)[1]

Naturally, people disagreed, but Wiliam is no fringe thinker. He's a widely-respected British academic with a focus on teaching and learning. Here are two internationally respected cognitive scientists saying essentially the same thing:

---

1   bit.ly/3D5nVIy

Learning is a change in long-term memory.

Those scientists would be Paul A. Kirschner and Carl Hendrick writing in 2020's *How Learning Happens: Seminal Works in Educational Psychology and What They Mean in Practice* (pg. 172). While *How Learning Happens* is a great book and one we recommend, if you have time for only one book on the subject of memory and learning, for our money *Make It Stick* is the best. Rather than straightforward recitation of facts, it's centered around stories. As Willingham noted in *Why Don't Students Like School?* stories are privileged in memory, and so *Make It Stick* is designed to, well, make it stick.

One of our favorite quotes from *Make It Stick* is this:

> Memorizing facts is like stocking a construction site with the supplies to put up a house. Building the house requires not only knowledge of countless different fittings and materials but conceptual understanding...Mastery requires both the possession of ready knowledge and the conceptual understanding of how to use it (pp. 18-19).

This metaphor comparing learning to construction isn't new. In the *Nicomachean Ethics*, Aristotle says, "as you will become a good builder from building well, so you will become a bad one from building badly. Were this not so, there would be no need for teachers of the arts, but everybody would be born a good or bad craftsman as the case might be."

What these thinkers all agree on is that memory is the heart of learning. We can't think about what we don't know. Most adults would agree that we continue learning throughout our lives, and that learning isn't always easy or natural. More often, learning takes effort.

Working Memory vs. Long-Term Memory

Keeping in mind that these are concepts from models of the brain and not meant to reflect actual parts of your brain, there are two key ideas from cognitive science for our purposes: working (or short-term) memory and long-term memory.

Working memory is the part of the brain where people temporarily store information and work with it. Scientists know that working memory is limited and brief. How limited? Between four and seven items at a time. How brief? About 30 seconds.[2] Gifted students can often hold more in working memory and hold information longer, while students with attention and memory

---

2   Kirschner, P and Hendrick, C (2020) *How Learning Happens: Seminal Works in Educational Psychology and What They Mean in Practice*, Routledge.

problems tend to have less holding capacity and less time with material. It's well known that anxiety, anger, and fatigue reduce working memory, while calm, curiosity, and happiness increase working memory.

The second key idea is long-term memory. Many cognitive scientists view long-term memory as the central feature of our minds—we are what we know, and we know what we remember. The key for educators of all kinds is to *help learners know things*. For our purposes, long-term memory is where the concepts of domain-specific knowledge, skills, and abilities come into play. For example, just because you know how to change a tire doesn't mean that you know how to change diapers. Those are domain-specific pieces of information in long-term memory—and they're not "just facts."

In *Why Don't Students Like School?* Daniel Willingham reminds us that your long-term memory contains both facts and procedures. What is a procedure? A procedure is how to do things. The steps in long division or parallel parking your car are procedures. These procedures are often clunky, and many people derisively refer to them as mere algorithms. However, stocking your long-term memory with procedures improves the quality of your thinking. I know that when the right front bumper of the car behind me is in the middle of the rear of my car in the rear-view mirror, then it's time to cut my wheels so that I don't end up with a multi-thousand dollar repair bill at the autobody shop. That's an algorithm, and it's good thinking!

Facts and procedures stored in long-term memory can be called into consciousness at will, making them available for use by the working memory when faced with a new, perplexing situation. And that's exactly what we want students to be able to do with their learning: solve novel problems. That's part of what most people mean when they refer to "critical thinking."

Bridging the Gap: Cognitive Load and Chunking

Along with the distinctions between working and long-term memory, a key idea from cognitive science is *cognitive load*. Cognitive load as a testable cognitive science theory was put forth by John Sweller in the mid-1980s.[3] In this theory, *mental effort* is a combination of task complexity, learner expertise, self-efficacy, and information processing. In short, if the work is too hard, if your child doesn't have enough relevant background information, if your child doesn't believe they can do the work, or your child cannot understand the problem, then your child won't be able to do the work.

---

3   Sweller J (1988) "Cognitive Load During Problem Solving: Effects on Learning", *Cognitive Science*, 12(2) 257-285.

This might seem obvious, but this is a key research paper in cognitive science, and the results have been repeated many times. Why is it so important? Because relevant background information matters—there is no such thing as "general critical thinking skills." How much does relevant background information matter? The key difference between a novice and an expert in a field is how much background knowledge they have. The technical term for this is "memory of problem state configurations"[4] and the classic study for this is about chess players. Expert chess players have memorized thousands of game board patterns and use those memories to make good choices to win the game. However, this idea about how we solve problems has been replicated across fields from art to insurance to brain surgery.[5]

For example, Courtney once was leading a Girl Scout meeting, and the girls were to illustrate a zoo. She had a scout who'd *never been to a zoo*. The scout had no frame of reference for how zoos were laid out in winding paths or that there were stops built into the paths for people to look at the animals. Without that background knowledge, the scout was relegated to adding glitter to other people's work. Nobody wants their child to be limited to adding glitter—so build that background knowledge.

Remember that cognitive load is not only dependent on background knowledge. Task complexity matters, too. This is where inquiry-based teaching falls down on the job. By giving our learners too few guidelines, problem-based curricula overwhelm our children with enormous demands on their working memory as they frantically try to figure out what to do next. Your child can't independently solve the problem of writing an essay on World War II if they don't know about World War II and don't know how to write an essay. The very act of trying to figure out what to do means that they don't have space in their limited working memory to funnel information into long-term memory. And again, funneling information into long-term memory is the very definition of learning. Knowledge first, then problem solving.

Self-efficacy, or believing that you can do the work, also matters. Homeschoolers have an advantage because we tend to have good relationships with our children and can encourage them to solve more difficult problems through praise and rewards. "You can do this, sweetheart! Give me five more correct math problems, and we'll stop for ten minutes and pick up with history."

---

4 Kirschner, P and Hendrick, C (2020).

5 Brown, P C, Roediger, H L and McDaniel, M A (2014) *Make It Stick: The Science of Successful Learning*, Harvard University Press.

Chunking for Schemas

Information processing is a more complicated part of cognitive load theory. One way we can process information is to "chunk" little pieces of information together to make it easier to remember. For example, when Courtney was a little girl, her family's answering machine code was 1397, the four corners of the phone touch pad. Rather than remember the numbers, she remembered to use the corners. Each chunk occupies one part of working memory. In other words, rather than remembering the telephone number 263-464-1397, she can easily hold the word CODING and then the idea of four corners in her limited working memory while she dialed the number—only two bits of information instead of ten.

Since working memory is limited, it represents "a fundamental bottleneck of human cognition" (*Why Don't Students Like School?* pg. 121). Despite what some snake oil sellers on the Internet may promise, there have been no reputable studies that demonstrate improvement in working memory through some kind of treatment. You get what you get, and you don't get upset. However, chunking is one way to maximize the working memory we have. By chunking, we can make a word take the same amount of room in working memory as an individual letter, freeing up space for more learning.

Automaticity is the single best way to free space in working memory. I don't have to think about every single aspect of driving to the grocery store—I can listen to music, hold a conversation, and so on because I've learned how to drive so well that it's automatic. Likewise, fluent reading is automatic reading, which is why fluent readers are faster readers. It's much quicker to just "know" something—to be able to effortlessly access it from long-term memory— than it is to have to stop and think about what you're reading. Math facts operate the same way. Rather than straining our working memory, we will just know that 5 x 7 is 35, whether we're trying to figure it out or not. That's what automatic means.

We can use chunks to build *schemas*, or the organization of how information is related. For example, most of us remember that all email addresses have an initial part, the "@" symbol, a domain name, and then an end code: example@test.com. If someone gave you their email address, but simply said "at Gmail," your memorized chunks of common email address endings would cause you to recall that Gmail addresses end with .com and thus satisfy the schema for how email addresses should be arranged.[6]

As Willingham notes, background knowledge goes far beyond recall of simple

---

6 For more on schemas, see Efrat Furst's excellent Google site, *Learning in the Brain.*

facts. Schemas also include much more complex ideas that have been effectively chunked and stored in long-term memory, like the algorithm for long division. Willingham writes, "It's not just facts that reside in memory; solutions to problems, complex ideas you've teased apart, and conclusions you've drawn are also part of your store of knowledge." This is one way that knowledge actually improves not just reading comprehension, but that holy grail of Western education, analytical thinking.

And in some domains, Willingham says, knowledge in schemas is much more important than reasoning or problem-solving abilities. When Drew is tutoring a student in a foreign language or literature, they're much more likely to call upon their knowledge of grammar or history or literary terms than on any sort of problem-solving. Drew would go so far as to say that the more experienced a teacher is in their field, the less problem-solving they have to do. If a student is struggling, an experienced teacher can often recognize the source of the problem and offer a solution based on what's worked in the past—the teacher has a schema for the student's difficulty. This in itself is an application of memory, albeit a more complex one than just knowing a simple fact.

Interestingly, some people think that knowledge alone can raise your IQ.[7] This is a subject that Willingham touches on in the newest edition of *Why Don't Students Like School?* Didau believes so strongly in the power of a knowledge rich curriculum to raise IQ and thus improve a child's life, he's written an entire book about it, called *Making Kids Cleverer* (2019).

Exposure: We're Not Talking about the South Side of the House

We need to say a word about exposure. Last week, Jenn took her youngest to the planetarium. As they toured the museum, he recognized several pieces of information from earlier studies. Does that mean that he doesn't need any more work with that information? Not at all.

As Drew says, Jenn's youngest had passive knowledge, not active knowledge. When information is passive, you have been exposed to it, but as Daniel Willingham says, it's *inflexible*. You can recall it, but only in certain situations. If we were building a house, these are pieces waiting on the ground under a tarp, not yet integrated as part of the supporting structure. Passive vocabulary is understood, but you don't use it in your own speech or writing.

---

7   Ritchie, S J and Tucker-Drob, E M (2018) "How Much Does Education Improve Intelligence? A Meta-Analysis", *Psychological Science*, 29(8) 1358-1369.

When knowledge is active, you've fully integrated it into your schema. Now, the information supports your mental architecture, and you can and will use it on a regular basis. Vocabulary is obvious, but this integration works for ideas, concepts, and procedures. Quick, how many planets are there? If you're older, like we are, you will have to pause and remember that there are now eight, because our schemas were built with nine.

This is not to say that all knowledge has to be active in your mind. A great deal of it can be a *known unknown*, sufficient for E. D. Hirsch, Jr.'s idea of cultural literacy—or, as Drew's friend Nicole says, to get jokes that assume a knowledge of pre-21st-century experience. We cannot all be experts in everything, with fully automated chunks in deeply complex schemas, and that's fine.

Filling the Memory Banks for Better Learning

How many bits of information can our brains store in long-term memory? How many bits can our brains store in chunks? How many chunks? How many schemas? Humans have not reached the limit of long-term memory. Functionally, our long-term memory is unlimited.

In short, memorizing things expands children's long-term memories and expands their schemas, making better use of their limited short-term memory. For children on the lower end of the working memory scale, memorization is critical for problem solving, because those children can't afford to figure it out as they go—their working memory doesn't permit them the time or space. To quote the shoe giant Nike, these children need to be able to "just do it," or they'll forget what they're doing in the middle of a lengthy question.

ADHD brains have attention regulation problems and autistic brains often have difficulty with executive functioning. In our experience teaching autistic children and children with ADHD, we find the more knowledge is memorized, the easier studying is for those children. There is something to be gained by automatic retrieval. You don't have to struggle to stay on task if those facts are just there for you.

What about, as many folks argue, you know, just Googling it? If all the information in the world is on the Internet, why not just look it up? Well, for one thing, our brains are not calculators, or even computers. Working memory is a *model* for our brain, not reality. We do not have RAM chips or solid state hard drives in our heads. Because of the way our brains work, we need to know something for ourselves before we can make use of it.

Two Paths to Rule Them All

Sweller proposed that information moved from working memory to long-term memory through two main paths: auditory and visual. Basically, when children are distracted by background music or busy pages, their cognitive load is increased and they don't learn as well. Obviously, distracted people don't learn as well, you say. But wait, this particular model of the brain does have some useful information!

Auditory Input

According to Sweller's model, sound is processed separately from visual input. This means that if you're talking while your child is reading, there is excess cognitive load and they won't learn as well. They've actually tested this, and it's called the "split-attention effect." Essentially, remove competing stimuli. Don't let your child study while they listen to music (with exceptions for children with ADHD, for example). Don't expect your child to remember what you're saying if they're busy doing something else.

On the other hand, this idea that auditory input is just as important as visual input leads to the idea that children can use auditory input to help learn information. While old-school chanting is out of fashion in modern educational practices, chanting does work for many children!

Even commercial vendors have gone against the current fashion for all visual input of serious academics. For example, Times Tales is famously helpful for memorizing the multiplication tables. Young children and another language? Song School Spanish. There are even super specific items, such as the quadratic formula set to "Pop Goes the Weasel," or CrossSeven for Claritas memory work.

Importantly, children with ADHD or other issues often do not find these helpful. Know your child before embarking on song memorization.

Visual Input

One of the most famous and frequently tested consequences of cognitive load is the use of worked examples. These are most common in math programs, but you'll find them elsewhere. The instructor or textbook shows a problem solved step-by-step, minimizing the difficulty levels between steps.

Diagrams of concepts are often helpful, but they can actually be more *difficult* than a straightforward explanation when they're numbered and you have to go find what the numbers correspond to. Integrating the information into one diagram helps your child learn better. Better yet, put an entire written explanation within the diagram itself. Put the names of the countries on the map, instead of in a key.

What about videos or live demonstrations? If you keep the explanation clear and simple, like an elegant Instagram reel for a cooking demonstration, then a video is superior to a diagram. Pre-loading information in orderly chunks before integrating multiple steps in a video or live demonstration is also useful. "This is a tire. This is a lug nut. This is a jack. This is a wrench. Now, watch as I use them to change the tire."

Memorization Is Not a Dirty Word

All of this is to say you must make students memorize facts, procedures, and concepts. One might even say that teaching is leading students through memorization. Memorizing simply means moving information from working memory to long-term memory.

Memorization is not a dirty word, and we shouldn't confuse it with "rote learning." Learning by rote means learning something *without context or understanding*. That's obviously not what we're going for. We want that information fully integrated in schemas. And don't fall for the line that students need conceptual understanding, not memorization. They need both, but they quite literally cannot achieve understanding without a base of facts to work with. Daniel Willingham explains this well in his book *Why Don't Students Like School?*

The important key to putting this to work in your homeschool is to make memorization not too hard and not too easy. Aim for the Goldilocks zone, and your children will feel good naturally, even when they don't particularly love the content.[8] How do we find the Goldilocks zone? When your child whines to finish that YouTube video, there are dirty dishes in the sink, the cat is sitting on the clean laundry still in the basket, and your toddler is banging on the window, we're hard pressed to customize lessons to our child's exact skill level.

Some things are harder to memorize than others. Sheer exposure means that the average 3-year-old knows the McDonald's logo, but students typically aren't exposed to the academic content we want them to learn every time we drive somewhere. The French neuroscientist Stanislas Dehaene uses the following analogy to illustrate the difficulty in memorizing addition ("lives on") and multiplication ("works on") tables. (Zoe is 0, Albert is 1, Bruno is 2, etc.)

- *Charlie David lives on George Avenue*
- *Charlie George lives on Albert Zoe Avenue*
- *George Ernie lives on Albert Bruno Avenue*

---

8   For more on this idea, see *Flow* by Mihaly Csikszentmihalyi (1990).

- *Charlie David works on Albert Bruno Avenue*
- *Charlie George works on Bruno Albert Avenue*
- *George Ernie works on Charlie Ernie Avenue*[9]

If this is confusing, so are the multiplication tables to your average 8- or 9-year-old. But there is more to the world than multiplication tables. In chapter three of *The Well-Trained Mind*, the authors mention what psychologists call frequency bias. You notice something and suddenly you see it everywhere. As the authors of *The Well-Trained Mind* note, frequency bias is good for learning because it allows you to build a schema around the piece of information.

We want to work with our children to help expand their knowledge base. For example, Courtney made a set of T-shirt dresses for her youngest this spring, based on the days of the week. Sun-day, Moon-day, Mars-Day, Odins-Day, Thors-Day, Frigga-day, and Saturn-day. Suddenly, her youngest child saw information about space everywhere! On Mars-day, she would wear her dress with a cartoon axolotl sitting on top of the red planet and remember that Mars is red because of the rust in its soil. She was expanding her schema based on what the authors of *The Well-Trained Mind* call "mental pegs on which later information can be hung."[10]

One of the reasons we like spiral curricula (a tight spiral, not the yearly exposure type), is because, as Willingham says, "The surest way to help students understand an abstraction is to expose them to many different versions of the abstraction" (*Why Don't Students Like School?*, pg. 96). We swing back around to the information or concept again and again and again. Saxon math is notorious for the tight spiral, swinging back around to reteach concepts in more depth every three to five weeks, while continuing practice with older concepts. Swinging back around is also the rationale for the neoclassical four-year history cycle, repeating ancient history in first, fifth, and ninth grades.

Good teachers teach by analogy to known information, enlarging schemas as they go. Fingers are to hands as toes are to? If algebra is arithmetic, we can confidently assure our children who've completed an elementary arithmetic program that they already know how to do everything we're going to teach them. We're just going to account for variables—and we do. All year long, it's "remember when you learned how to do X? Well, we're going to do that now, just with variables!"

Analogies are not enough, however. Children need concrete, familiar examples.

9   Dehaene, S (2011) *The Number Sense: How the Mind Creates Mathematics*, Oxford University Press.

10   Wise. J and Bauer Wise, S (1999).

That's where math manipulatives come in handy, or letter tiles when they're learning to read, or demonstrations in science. By the way, Oliver Caviglioli does a great job at showing how we can make the abstract concrete in his book *Dual Coding With Teachers*. Willingham argues:

> It's not the concreteness, it's the familiarity that's important; but most of what students are familiar with is concrete, because abstract ideas are so hard to understand. Understanding new ideas is mostly a matter of getting the right old ideas into working memory and then rearranging them— making comparisons we hadn't made before, or thinking about a feature we had previously ignored (*Why Don't Students Like School?* pg. 99).

Because we're so familiar with our own children, we have an advantage here. We tend to know what they know, and so we can give them examples with which they're already familiar to better help them learn.

Making It Stick: Retrieval Practice

Sewing a week's worth of dresses to help create mental pegs to hang information on isn't a skill that everyone has, so how can you help your children memorize the vast quantities of information needed to succeed in modern society? As Kirschner and Hendrick note, the two best techniques for teacher implementation are spaced retrieval practice—"small, frequent homework assignments that include new and previously treated material, cumulative tests, short review sessions at the beginning of the lesson, spiral curriculum, etc."—and the testing effect, including "quizzes, practice tests, and review questions."[11]

Especially with neurodivergent children, you can only be sure of what your children know if you assess their knowledge regularly. A bird unit study is fun and lovely, but unless you quiz your children at the end and see what they actually remember, you don't know if they learned anything. No prompting either! No "Tommy, remember when we went to the aviary?" They have to know it for themselves, or they don't know it. Retrieval practice helps them keep information accessible in their memory.

Can't we just learn something and be done with it? Does this seem like an unnecessary hassle? As classroom teachers regularly sigh, you cannot assume that children will understand or remember what they studied even last week! In fact, they probably won't unless you have explicitly and systematically reviewed the material at given intervals. The testing effect means that simply quizzing

---

11   Kirschner, P and Hendrick, C (2020).

learners on material at regular intervals makes them recall the information and cement it into their mind. Good curricula will do this for you, but even then, you need to follow through.

Let's be frank, asking a homeschooler to create an interwoven set of assignments while designing a high-quality curriculum from scratch is like plopping a high school band student in a professional musician's studio and expecting them to write an orchestral score. Interweaving all these complex threads of learning for retrieval practice is not an easy task. That's why we suggest borrowing someone else's plan. In particular, Drew has written a resource designed to help homeschoolers provide their children with a general set of background information, called *Living Memory*.

The flip side is, as *Make It Stick* says, "[S]tudents who don't quiz themselves (and most do not) tend to overestimate how well they have mastered class material." This is why just asking "Did you get that? Do you understand?" doesn't cut it. We all laughed at Ben Stein in *Ferris Bueller's Day Off*, but we're all guilty of just going on and not quizzing all our children and making sure they give us the actual answer. Checking for understanding is a critical step of your teaching process.

Flashcards Are Good, Actually

A good curriculum will emphasize practice of processes that need to become automatic for students. For example, all those Saxon math problems will help students overlearn and automate their skills, and the tight spiral will help space out practice for better recall on those standardized  tests in the spring. Those 30 lessons on nouns in *First Language Lessons, Level 1* use auditory input and overlearning to ensure that your child never forgets the definition of a noun. Pop quiz time: Do you remember the definition of a noun? No? Maybe it's time to pick up a copy of *First Language Lessons!*

For custom memorization work, have children implement a Leitner box. Sebastian Leitner was a German scientist who developed a system for spaced practice of flashcards. While software does exist that automatically shuffles cards based on Ebbinghaus' forgetting curve and Leitner's algorithm, not all families can afford the tech. Most families can lay hands on index cards, pencils, and plastic baggies to keep cards sorted.

Typically, children would write the week's memory work on a flash card — the order of the planets in the Solar System, Henry VIII's wives, or this week's multiplication facts: 3rd planet from the Sun—Earth; Henry VIII's first wife—Catherine of Aragon; 3 x 7 = 21.

Then, on the first day, your children would review the flashcards. The items they missed would go in group one, reviewed daily. The items they answered correctly would go into group two, which is reviewed less often, possibly Monday/Wednesday/Friday. Then on Wednesday, they would review their daily cards (again, cards they know are bumped down to group two), and the group two cards. Known group two cards are bumped down to group three. Unknown group two cards are bumped back to daily. Group three cards are reviewed weekly. Similarly, if group three cards are known, they are bumped down to group four, and if they are unknown, they are bumped back to group two. Group four cards are reviewed once a month. If they are missed, they are bumped back to group three. Group four is never bumped down—reviewing known material once a month makes it stick indefinitely.

If that sounds confusing, here is a sample monthly calendar:

Monday	Tuesday	Wednesday	Thursday	Friday
Group one Group two	Group one	Group one Group two	Group one Group three	Group one Group two
Group one Group two	Group one	Group one Group two	Group one Group three	Group one Group two
Group one Group two	Group one	Group one Group two	Group one Group three	Group one Group two
Group one Group two	Group one Group four	Group one Group two	Group one Group three	Group one Group two

As your children memorize the information, it gradually moves to the back of their recitation schedule, but never entirely disappears. At the end of the year, your children have built up a considerable body of knowledge with individualized practice based on their own interleaved, interval-spaced retrieval practice. Practice also helps with students being able to transfer problem solving skills between slightly different problems.

Shuffling cards back and forth between the groups in the box helps interleave the cards to provide discrimination practice, allowing students to quickly select the right answer among a small group of choices. Dumping all their different classes in one box varies the practice, which helps students "build a broad schema, an ability to assess changing conditions and adjust responses to fit."[12]

---

12 Brown, P C, Roediger, H L and McDaniel, M A (2014).

Memorization in Reading

Think about what it's like teaching a child to read. You've probably watched your child strain their working memory so much just by sounding out the words that they completely miss the meaning of what they just read. It's only after they've learned to chunk all the graphemes in their long-term memory for quick recall that they easily read a sentence aloud and understand the meaning. Good direct-instruction curricula carefully scaffold that memorization sequence to help your children learn to decode the English language.

Research implies that "integrated literacy and content-area instruction has potential to enhance vocabulary words taught to students and comprehension in the elementary years, with the additional benefit of simultaneously cultivating science and social studies knowledge."[13] Core Knowledge, *Story of the World*, *Exploring the World through Story*, and many other programs have an explicit focus on integrated literacy and content-area instruction.

Memorization in Math

Working memory and background knowledge matter for math, too. Children who have not memorized their multiplication tables are frustrated in learning long division because by the time they stop and figure out 8 x 7, they have lost their place in the problem. Moreover, a deep comfort with long division is essential for later success in algebra.

Both students and teachers are frustrated when key background knowledge is missing, making improbable requests of tasks like long division, adding rational expressions with unlike denominators, or calculating probability. In fact, mathematics is so powerfully predicated on previous knowledge that it is one of the few subjects in the United States with a clearly delineated progression of knowledge building. Second languages are usually the other subject.

For example, many of us grew up with pre-algebra, then algebra, then geometry (usually for the knowledge to do well on college admissions tests), then algebra II. Some differences occur at this point (Courtney took Algebra III), but most college-bound students will take trigonometry, and then perhaps calculus. Integrated high school mathematics follows a similar progression, albeit with more statistics and less coverage of other topics, such as arithmetic operations

---

13 Hwang, H, Cabell S Q and Joyner R E (2021) "Effects of Integrated Literacy and Content-area Instruction on Vocabulary and Comprehension in the Elementary Years: A Meta-analysis", *Scientific Studies of Reading*, 26(3) 223-249.

on polynomials. These are bright line standards for what students should know and when they should know it and, unfortunately, are almost never implemented in other subjects. We know what algebra II looks like, but what is an equivalent level in reading? History? Geography? Biology? (Unless you were like Courtney and were lucky enough to take Biology II.)

To end this chapter, we're going to give you a summary as well as a list of key terms and their meanings. Before you read the next paragraph, try to write down as many facts and definitions from this chapter as you can remember. This technique is called a "brain dump" and is one method frequently used for retrieval practice.

How did you do? This exercise shows you how challenging it is for our children to understand and retain information from their reading. (And remember, kids are usually not as skilled in reading as adults!) Ready for a review? Read on.

Summary

Learning is memorization. We use working memory to funnel new information into long-term memory. Information includes facts, concepts, and procedures. Long-term memory supplies our short-term memory with information to solve problems. Because working memory is limited, the cognitive load of a given task restricts the ability to move information into long-term memory. We can evade this limitation by chunking information and relating information with schemas. Complex, well-developed schemas lead to increased problem-solving ability. Not all schemas need to be well-developed for our children to learn. Our long-term memory storage is unlimited, which is helpful for problem-solving skills. We primarily move information into long-term memory through auditory and visual input. Memory work at the correct level of difficulty can be provided through good curricula, a supportive environment, good teaching, and retrieval practice. Retrieval practice is most commonly frequent, low-stakes quizzing integrated into the learning process, such as flashcards. Achievement in reading and math is dependent on memorization.

- **Automaticity**: Learning something until it's fully integrated into a schema; able to be used without strain on working memory or succumbing to recall failure.

- **Background knowledge**: Facts, procedures (how something is done), and concepts (ideas); provides necessary foundation for problem-solving skills.

- **Chunking**: Joining pieces of information into a single, functional unit in long-term memory.

- **Cognitive load**: The strain on your working memory from the combination of task complexity, learner expertise levels, self-efficacy, and information processing abilities.

- **Ebbinghaus' forgetting curve**: A model that demonstrates how memories are lost over time but can be kept by spaced retrieval practice.

- **Leitner box**: Box of flashcards designed to use the Ebbinghaus' forgetting curve for increased memorization.

- **Long-term memory**: The part of the brain which holds the concepts of domain-specific knowledge, skills, and abilities; unlimited storage.

- **Memorization**: Learning.

- **Retrieval practice**: Low-stakes, frequent quizzing using spaced practice.

- **Schemas**: A complex, integrated unit of learning.

- **Working memory**: The part of the brain where people temporarily store information and work with it; fixed bottleneck in human learning; auditory and visual components.

CHAPTER 8
NOTES ON READING, SPELLING, AND HANDWRITING

This is the first of three chapters on English Language Arts (ELA), a subject that consists of multiple instructional areas. This chapter talks about reading and its inverse, spelling, as well as handwriting, since handwriting is often taught concurrently with phonics in grades K–2. The next chapter will deal with composition (a.k.a. "writing"), and the one after that, with the remaining subjects under the ELA umbrella: vocabulary, grammar, and literature.

Teaching Your Child to Read

Teaching your child to read is perhaps the most difficult and most important job you will ever have as a homeschooling parent. Achieving basic fluency in reading English is a complex, multi-part operation that in our experience takes a minimum of 30 months, but more commonly requires up to five years. You'll need multiple passes through material offered by widely different curricula to develop knowledge, skills, and abilities for reading that are more complex than merely decoding the English alphabet—and this is the standard for a typically developing student. If your student is neurodivergent or has learning disabilities, this process can be even more difficult and can take much longer.

Dr. Hollis Scarborough, a reading researcher, explains the complexity of this task with the image of *the reading rope*. Her analogy is that learning to read requires eight interwoven skill strands for children to become fluent readers. Only when all eight strands (skills) are mastered can a child be considered a competent reader.

Scarborough's Reading Rope in Action

Word Recognition

1. **Phonological Awareness**

   Fortunately, the first steps are probably something you already do as a parent. For example, phonological awareness is frequently introduced with nursery rhymes. "Hickory dickory dock, the mouse ran up the clock." Rhyming stories like *Sheep in a Jeep* and *Llama Llama Red Pajama* are both enjoyable for young children and invaluable for their future reading skills.

Just being able to hear syllables in words like "chick-en," "ba-na-na," and "cat-er-pil-lar," is important. Hearing syllables is also great fun when you play with sound repetition or alliterations. "Oops sounds like loops." "Betty Botter bought a bit of butter..." Those tongue twisters are perfect.

2. Decoding

These foundational skills lead nicely into decoding. Luckily, there are great curricula to teach your kids to decode. If one doesn't suit you, get another one. The classic, best selling book since 1986, is *Teach Your Child to Read in 100 Easy Lessons*. Generations of children have learned to read with this book. There's also *The Ordinary Parents Guide to Teaching Reading*, which takes you all the way through fourth grade phonics. Yes, dear reader, there is a fourth grade phonics. *The Logic of English* is super popular, super thorough, and has a special strand for children who are a little bit older but not reading well. *All About Reading* is an excellent direct instruction program for those children who might need some extra support. An old, but still quite useful program is *Phonics Pathways*. While less babyish than other programs, it doesn't have much instructor hand holding.

Those are just a handful of popular curricula. There are more available, and we recommend that you buy a copy of *The Well-Trained Mind* and do some reading. Some curricula are free, and some are quite expensive. If you have a child with severe dyslexia, a Barton tutor implementing the Orton-Gillingham system used to be the best program. However, it is exceedingly expensive. Recently, we learned of the SPIRES program. The third edition is available for sale to homeschoolers and can be implemented by the parent, saving money.

3. Sight Reading

While an Orton-Gillingham trained tutor would vehemently disagree, we do think that a tiny bit of sight word recognition practice will make your child's life easier. For example, the word "the" can be taught through decoding, but it's so common that your child might pick it up all by themselves. To ease that process slightly, the *Bob* books and the *Dick and Jane* books are classic helps. Again, these are not a substitute for direct instruction for decoding, but a temporary band-aid on the path to reading acquisition.

Language Comprehension

1. Background Knowledge

Beyond a knowledge-rich direct instruction curriculum, we can provide children with a wealth of diffuse background knowledge. One way we can do that is by taking your child out into the world with field trips to museums, art galleries, and so on. Drawing on Courtney's experience with Birth to Three, we think that talking with your child is possibly the single most important intervention you can do with young children. Erica Christakis wrote an entire book about the critical value of interacting with young children, *The Importance of Being Little* (2016).

Teaching children to notice and wonder is another key skill. In classical education, you'll find deliberate inclusion of "picture study." As we discussed earlier, our vision system is one of the two main ways that children access the world around them. Deliberately and systematically teaching children to notice details and make inferences from images is worthwhile.

One of the major parts of building knowledge for good reading comprehension is, as E. D. Hirsch, Jr. says, "a systematic curriculum that presents new words in familiar context, thereby enabling students to make correct meaning guesses unconsciously." Or, alternatively, a view of knowledge building from Susan Wise Bauer, who says, "In the content areas of history, science, literature, art, and music, classical learning provides a systematic framework for learning about new things."

2. Vocabulary

Vocabulary is another key component of Scarborough's rope. Typically, we begin formal vocabulary study in two ways, through content discussion and through formal spelling curricula. As children get older, spelling moves into vocabulary study and what we might recognize as Structured Word Inquiry. Essentially, we should show children how words break down into parts and then reform as new words. This means we show children root words, suffixes, and prefixes, and demonstrate those across the curriculum.

There are many accessible spelling and vocabulary curricula for homeschoolers. Personally, we have used and enjoyed *Spelling Workout, All About Spelling, Vocabulary from Classical Roots, Sadlier,* and *Wordly Wise.*

3. Language Structures

These include grammar and composition, which we discuss in depth elsewhere. Two curricula that are a personal favorite for the early elementary age are *Writing With Ease* and *First Language Lessons*. As per our earlier discussion, handwriting and composition are not the same thing. We may choose to teach them in concert, but they're separate subjects. There are good curricula for handwriting, and *The Well-Trained Mind* gives in-depth reviews of some of the best curricula for homeschoolers. Personally, we have used and enjoyed *Handwriting Without Tears, The Logic of English: the Rhythm of Handwriting*, and *Getty-Dubay*. Jenn is such a fan of *Getty-Dubay* that she's converted Courtney to using it in her homeschool.

4. **Verbal Reasoning**

As we discussed earlier, this typically falls under the purview of critical thinking, and there are specific curricula for this. In the early elementary stage, you might buy *Lollipop Logic, Logic Safari*, or *Logic Countdown*. Later, you might use *Building Critical Thinking Skills* or even think about the narration portion of *Writing With Ease*.

5. **Literacy Knowledge**

One of the nice parts of *Writing With Ease* is that the included read-alouds use a variety of genres. In addition, it develops many of the foundational print concepts. We checked more than one book out of the library because our children wanted to hear the rest of the story.

When studying the neoclassical history cycle, Susan Wise Bauer points out, "The student who is working on ancient history will read Greek and Roman mythology, the tales of The Iliad and The Odyssey, early medieval writings, Chinese and Japanese fairy tales. Older students will read classic texts from Plato, Virgil, and Aristotle." By engaging with original works, students learn themes and patterns in later works. Eventually, they can mix and match these themes for their own, original work.

Background Knowledge Is Crucial

What exactly do we mean by "background knowledge"? Here's a good definition from Smith, Snow, Serry, and Hammond from their journal article, "The Role of Background Knowledge in Reading Comprehension." They say, "background knowledge comprises all of the world knowledge that the reader brings to the task of reading."

Knowing stuff matters across domains. If good background knowledge leads to better reading test scores, then better reading test scores imply higher test scores in general *because students know more stuff*—and this is borne out by the research. For example, high school students who test well in reading get better biology scores.[1] College students who tested poorly in reading but took a remedial reading class were more likely to graduate from college and had higher GPAs.[2] 4th and 5th graders who were good readers had higher standardized test scores across *content areas*, not just in reading.[3]

Even if we're not considering academic content, background knowledge matters. Here's a quote from a local paper:

> The Lions' last two losses have been punctuated by difficulties defending set pieces. At the start of the season, defense was their strong suit in these situations. Centerback Antonio Carlos was especially confident in aerial challenges, knocking away crosses to keep the box clear on designed plays. (Julia Poe, *Orlando Sentinel*, October 30, 2021)

Unless you're a soccer fan, that paragraph will probably mean nothing to you. Or take this explanation from E. D. Hirsch Jr.:

> Consider the following sentence, which is one that most literate Americans can understand but most literate English people cannot, even when they have a wide vocabulary and know the conventions of the standard language:
>
> *"Jones sacrificed and knocked in a run."*
>
> Typically, a literate English person would know all the words yet wouldn't comprehend the sentence. (In fairness, most Americans would be equally baffled by a sentence about the sport of cricket.) To understand this sentence about Jones and his sacrifice, you need a wealth of relevant background knowledge that goes beyond vocabulary and syntax—relevant knowledge that is far broader than the words of the sentence present (E. D. Hirsch, Jr. *The Knowledge Deficit*, 68-69).

Why does all this matter? Because reading is more than just accurate and automatic decoding. In their influential 1986 journal article, "Decoding, Reading, and Reading Disability," Tunmer and Gough proposed a model for reading comprehension, the "Simple View of Reading." In their article,

---

1   Allen, D A (2014) "A Test of the Relationship between Reading Ability & Standardized Biology Assessment Scores", *The American Biology Teacher*, 76(4) 247-251.

2   Gambino, Ellen M. (2012), "An Examination of the Relationship and Correlations Among Standardized Reading Test Scores, the Academic Success of Students, and the Completion of a Remedial Reading Course at a Mid-Sized Suburban Community College."

3   Alley, J (2012) "The Impact of Reading Achievement on Standardized Testing," Northwest Missouri State University, Research Paper.

Tunmer and Gough give a formula that explains how reading works: *word recognition skills x language comprehension = reading comprehension.* (It's more complicated than that, of course, but all models are simplifications. That's why they're models, and not the real world. The map is not the terrain.)

One of the key findings in research about reading comprehension is that the more background knowledge you have, the more you can learn from your reading. Here's E. D. Hirsch, Jr., to explain:

> Many specialists estimate that a child or an adult needs to understand around 90 percent of the words in a passage in order to learn to understand the other 10 percent of the words. Moreover, it's not just the words that the student has to grasp the meaning of; it's also the kind of reality that the words are referring to. When a child doesn't understand those word meanings and those referred-to realities, being good at sounding out words is a dead end. Reading becomes a kind of Catch-22. In other words, in order to learn how to read with understanding, you already have to be able to read with understanding. [4]

There are many reasons that a child might not read well. They could be English Language Learners; nationwide in the USA, about one child in ten is learning English during compulsory attendance years. The child could have dyslexia; conservative estimates suggest that one student in 20 is dyslexic, with some estimates as high as one in nine. A child could have poor reading comprehension skills, or perhaps be visually impaired in some way.

Whatever the reasons, fully *two-thirds* of fourth graders are not proficient readers, and this is a consistent statistic over the years according to the NAEP studies. This means that in a typical US class of 24 students, two are learning English, one or two have dyslexia—and the majority of them are not good readers. We wish we could say that homeschoolers are immune to all this, but we're not. In fact, plenty of families homeschool *because* their children were struggling and not getting the help they needed in the public schools. On the other hand, we've also observed that many parents overestimate their children's reading ability.

How Not to Teach Reading

We frequently see parents say, "I can teach my child to read with sight words. Some children learn to read like this." Unfortunately, there are over a million words in the English language and a child is not going to be able to memorize each word, or even all the main words. Sight word reading gains ground deceptively fast at the earliest stages, but then falls behind as children switch

---

4   Hirsch, *The Knowledge Deficit*, 25.

from learning to read to reading to learn. Do not rely on sight words or the so-called Whole Language method to teach reading. Students need explicit instruction that helps them make the connection between the oral language they know and the written symbols for that language that appear on the page. That instruction is popularly known as "phonics." The Reading Wars are over, and explicit phonics instruction is the clear victor.

Similarly, some parents subscribe to the "better late than early" philosophy of teaching their children to read based on research from languages with shallow orthographies such as Spanish or Italian. This is misguided because English is notoriously difficult to learn. You can teach an average child to decode Spanish in weeks, versus the years required for English.

The logic here is inescapable—and common sense: Children who learn to read early will read more than their peers who start later. All of this practice has a snowball effect as children get older, and so these early readers become excellent at academics. This academic snowball is sometimes referred to as "the Matthew Effect," a term coined by sociologist Robert  Merton and applied to reading by Keith Stanovich in his 1986 paper for *Reading Research Quarterly*: "The Matthew effects in reading, some consequences of individual differences in the acquisition of literacy."[5] The term is a reference to Matthew 25:29 in the Christian New Testament—"For unto every one that hath shall be given, and he shall have abundance: but from him that hath not shall be taken away even that which he hath"—or, in more colloquial terms, "the rich get richer and the poor get poorer." Stanovich explains:

> The increased reading experiences of children who crack the spelling sound code early thus have important positive feedback effects. Such feedback effects appear to be potent sources of individual differences in academic achievement.

In short, there is no good reason to delay a child's reading instruction. Children with learning disabilities that affect reading will often benefit from more, not less, intensive instruction.

Motivation and Reading

One of Jenn's tricks for encouraging children to build reading fluency after they've learned to decode is to let them loose with something that they have a high

---

5   Stanovich, K E (1986) "Matthew Effects in Reading: Some Consequences of Individuals Differences in the Acquisition of Literacy", *Reading Research Quarterly* 21(4) 360-407

interest in. For one of Jenn's kids, it was the old *Animal Crossing* video game.s There were whole paragraphs of text to read in the game, and until the child achieved fluency, he had to rely on other family members to read him the text. This child wanted to read what to do next so he could progress in the game, and that motivated him to improve his own fluency. Your child might be motivated by a different medium. Maybe you need to provide a graphic novel or instructions for building something. The child's intrinsic motivation is the key to encouraging more and more fluent reading.

Handwriting

While learning to read and write is the subject of much contentious debate in education circles, it appears to us that learning to read and write *at the same time* has fairly conclusively been shown to be superior to learning to read and write separately, for the average child. That's why we're placing our discussion of handwriting alongside reading.

Before we go on to the reasons why we believe it's worthwhile to give handwriting (especially cursive) a place in your homeschool, we do want to note two special situations that may affect when and how you approach this subject.

The first is the very early reader. If you have a 3-year-old who is absolutely insistent on learning to read but doesn't have the fine motor skills to write letters, don't worry about it. Drew's daughter, who began learning to read at age 2 years and 9 months, didn't have the small motor skills to write at that age, so they provided her with toys and games to slowly build the grip strength and muscle control necessary to use a pencil until, at around age four-and-a-half, she was ready for handwriting instruction.

The second situation is the student with dysgraphia. Courtney's eldest child learned to read fluently at a more usual age, in preschool and kindergarten, but severe dysgraphia means that even now, ten years later, her handwriting hasn't progressed past the 4-to-6-year-old stage. She maxed out the decoding test by age eight, but she has immense difficulty with putting pen to paper for physiological reasons. There was no reason to deprive her of the gift of reading just because her physical abilities didn't line up with her cognitive abilities.

Benefits of Handwriting Instruction

The usefulness of teaching cursive is often highly debated in ivory tower circles, but in our experience, homeschoolers tend to teach it. There are several good reasons for this practice. First, learning cursive allows children to read the writing of adults who wrote (and may still write) in cursive. Several years ago, Courtney gave a college graduation card to a younger friend, and her friend handed it back and asked her to read it aloud because she could not read cursive. In addition, writing in cursive is significantly faster and more efficient than writing in manuscript (print), because the pencil leaves the paper less frequently. This makes cursive useful for taking notes.

While there are conflicting studies about keyboarding versus handwriting in taking notes, the current preponderance of the evidence suggests that, for the typical student, taking notes by hand is superior to taking notes on keyboards. Why? When children are skilled typists, they're fluent enough and fast enough to type every word they hear:

> In essence, the words go in their ears and out of their fingers and they process the information only at the phonemic level. If they use pen and paper, then — unless they've taken steno — they are required to paraphrase, abbreviate, and extract the important things that are said (i.e., separate the wheat from the chaff). As such they are more deeply processing what is being said and, thus, they remember and learn better. [6]

Moreover, research from 2020 shows that people learn faster and remember more when writing by hand versus using a keyboard, for the exact same information. The researchers, Askvik and van der Meer, attribute this to "the benefits of sensory-motor integration."[7]

Other research supports increased learning from handwriting versus keyboards or videos. Wiley and Rapp, of the Johns Hopkins University, published research last year showing that people learn to recognize letters much faster when they write them by hand, versus learning to type them or watch videos for recognition. Learning to spell new words and read unfamiliar words was "decisively" easier when people used handwriting.

Some students with motor control issues find it easier to write in cursive, again because the pencil leaves the paper less, so these students are less likely to "lose their place" on the paper. A significant amount of research shows that students with reading issues often have difficulties with letter recognition and phonemic awareness. Because cursive letters can only be written one way, cursive makes learning the alphabet and the corresponding sounds easier for these students.

---

6   Kirschner and Hendrick, *How Learning Happens*, 27.

7   The Importance of Cursive Handwriting Over Typewriting for Learning in the Classroom, 1.

The venerable *Bringing Words to Life: Robust Vocabulary Instruction*, by Beck, McKeown, and Kucan, includes an entire chapter on the relationship between handwriting and improving vocabulary. Many exercises for vocabulary instruction include handwriting, including exercises offered in *Bringing Words to Life*. The authors note that while there is not definitive evidence about the utility of writing in learning vocabulary, the evidence does point toward writing being useful. And, of course, vocabulary knowledge is directly related to reading comprehension skills.

Like math and reading, handwriting is one of the fundamental skills that underlie other knowledge acquisition. In order to engage with content knowledge, students read about it, discuss it, and then write about it, at nearly all age levels. Researchers call this "cognitive offloading," or writing down your thoughts so that you can "see" your thoughts, which Annie Murphy Paul tells us is useful for manipulating them as though they are physical objects. This, in turn, allows us to use "embodied cognition" to work with information—and of course the better we can work with knowledge, the more we learn. Read more in Paul's *The Extended Mind* (2021), and in Caviglioli's *Dual Coding with Teachers* (2019).

Without rapid acquisition of effortless, automatic handwriting skills, children are at a disadvantage, whether at home or at school. Therefore, homeschoolers should make teaching handwriting a priority.

What to Look for in a Handwriting Curriculum

When choosing handwriting programs for typically developing children, look for one that teaches children to recognize the different strokes that combine to make letters. As the French cognitive neuroscientist Stanislas Dehaene has explained, our brains repurpose pattern recognition areas to recognize letters. Learning to recognize those patterns in parts of letters is a key early step in that process. Letter recognition reliably predicts reading ability, even in the youngest students. Note, however, that identifying symmetry is a learned skill that is often not reliable until age 8 or 9, which is why young children often reverse their letters. This is not a cause for alarm unless it persists. (Letter reversal is also not a reliable sign of dyslexia, as is sometimes believed.)

Because young children do not have adult levels of fine motor control, they need to practice handwriting every day, usually for about 20 minutes per day. To accommodate their developing fine motor skills and the fact that young children's near vision is typically poorer than that of most adults, most handwriting programs have younger children practice with relatively large letters, often on paper with ruling an inch wide or more. That same paper often includes a middle guideline, and sometimes a lower guide for letters, like *g* and *y*, that drop below the bottom rule. Students who have more difficulty than average might benefit from high contrast black and white guidelines, and possibly raised lines. Jenn recommends the Abilitations brand "Hi-Write" paper, which you can find on Amazon and at specialty stores.

Several quality handwriting programs are available, but most of them offer insufficient practice on their own. Classical educators often rely on copywork to fill in the practice gap. Homeschoolers can "double dip" by having children practice writing items for memorization, such as spelling words, aphorisms, poems, geographic facts, and so on. By having younger children both encode (spelling the item correctly when writing, using dictation) and decode (reading prior to copying), they engage more deeply with the information than simply hearing it aloud and reciting the information back.

CHAPTER 9
NOTES ON COMPOSITION

You may think of "composition" primarily as the name of an introductory English course in college. We're using the term here to resolve an ambiguity in the more general term *writing*, which can refer to handwriting and to the art of creative writing, as well as to the academic forms of writing we're mainly concerned with here. To avoid any confusion, we'll use *composition* to refer to that last meaning of "writing."

Deep divisions exist among teachers of composition. Some teachers see writing primarily as a way of fostering children's creativity, while others focus on writing as a way to build critical thinking skills. For those who privilege creativity, building authorial voice and confidence are primary goals. Those prioritizing critical thinking, on the other hand, focus on clear structure and appropriate mechanics and usage. Although all three of us write fiction, for the purposes of home education, we are all on #TeamAcademicWriting.

Creative writing is an art, and one that, while valuable, is not something most adults need to master, any more than every adult needs to be a concert pianist or professional ballet dancer. Students should learn to appreciate creative writing—that's part of the study of literature—but that doesn't mean they need to become creative writers themselves, unless that's something that they want and that their families support. However, every adult needs to be able to order their thoughts and put them into clear prose, whether that's for the purpose of charting at a nursing station, writing a business proposal, or composing an essay for a college course. We therefore suggest a program that builds thinking and writing skills slowly and sequentially from kindergarten through the end of high school.

In the primary grades (K–2 or –3), students are still working hard to crack the phonetic code and to master the physical skill of handwriting. Just as literacy skills build on students' facility with spoken language, writing skills require students to be able to arrange and articulate their thoughts orally before they try to commit words to the page. This is *oral narration*. They also need practice with spelling and mechanics via *copywork*—accurately copying a prepared piece of writing—and they need practice with holding words in their heads and transferring them accurately to paper, for which we use *dictation*. These three techniques—narration, copywork, and dictation—form the core of composition instruction through at least grades 2 or 3, and we recommend continuing with dictation through grade 5. These foundational skills are vital if students are going to become competent writers, and they should not be skipped, although they can be accelerated for older beginners.

For the low, low price of $4, Susan Wise Bauer will walk you through an excellent exposition of the limitations of young children in regard to cognitive load and composition in her talk "A Plan for Teaching Writing." This is absolute gold and we think everyone should have a listen. The MP3 is available from *welltrainedmind.com*.

We think that students should begin oral narration practice no later than first grade, and they can get a running start by answering simple comprehension questions about read-alouds in kindergarten: "What happened to the last Billy Goat Gruff?" By the middle of second grade, children should be writing short narrations of their own. By "short," we mean 1–3 sentences. Students who skip this step find it difficult to elaborate on more complex readings—and elaboration is one of the critical ways to "make it stick." If we had a nickel for every time a parent came to us and told us their 7th or 8th grader could read a passage and understand the material but was unable to whip out a short written summary, we'd be relaxing on the beach on Grand Cayman right about now.

For most children, learning how to do something, especially something as complex and cognitively demanding as composition, is best done in small, sequential steps with copious practice. That's why we give our children scaffolds to hang their writing on, including, yes, the dreaded five-paragraph essay.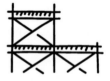

In *Teaching WalkThrus*, Sherrington and Caviglioli identify five steps for teaching: "1) present new material using small steps, 2) provide models, 3) provide scaffolds for difficult tasks, 4) ask questions, 5) check for student understanding." In step 3, those scaffolds include "modeling, checklists, writing frames, and anticipating errors and misconceptions." Experts don't need scaffolds because they already understand the deep structure of text, but our 13-year-olds are not experts. In the context of writing, this translates into a scaffolded curriculum with direct instruction, an emphasis on structure, and copious writing practice.

By the middle of elementary school, students should be producing some writing every school day, on topics drawn from the whole range of academic subjects: not just literature, but also social studies and science.

As Drew says, if you want your children to learn how to write well, you have to teach them how to do it, slowly, explicitly, and incrementally over the whole course of their schooling.[1] Having them do freewrites or dictations, as some popular homeschool programs do, is simply not enough to assure mastery. The conventional skills progression—sentence composition, paragraph formation, essays—forms the bridge to expertise for students. There's a reason that generations of English teachers have explicitly taught those skills and in that order.

When classical educators talk about "teaching children how to think," this is what they mean. You want to give your child exercises that inculcate orderly thought. In composition, this is making outlines, learning how to structure a paragraph, expanding the paragraph into an essay,[2] understanding how to construct a logically sound argument, and leading a reader through it.

And no, our students can't just ask Google how to write essays. We can find all kinds of things on the Internet, but Courtney would like to remind you about the notorious octopus study. In a study at the University of Connecticut, the vast majority of eighth-grade students fell for a hoax website about tree octopuses. Researchers blamed the lack of generic reading skills, but as we know from the baseball study (see chapter 17), the real problem was that students lacked the necessary scientific background knowledge to recognize that *octopuses can't live in trees*. They couldn't push back against false information without reliable background knowledge.

Whether your child is destined to be a Pulitzer prize-winning author or a gas well tender filling out their daily reports, we think basic writing skills, like constructing a paragraph or a report, are too valuable to be left to Google. The best way to build confidence in writing, as with everything else, is to build concrete skills, systematically and incrementally. Confidence follows competence.

---

1   For an outline of how to approach writing instruction, see Drew's article "Writing Instruction, Step by Step": quidnampress.com/writing-instruction-step-by-step.

2   See quidnampress.com/how-to-teach-essay-writing for a detailed explanation of this process, which will also be taught in the forthcoming middle school levels of Drew's world literature curriculum, *Exploring the World Through Story*.

CHAPTER 10
NOTES ON VOCABULARY, GRAMMAR, AND LITERATURE

In the last two chapters, we've covered reading, spelling, handwriting, and composition. This chapter will round out the list of ELA topics. We'll discuss some effective ways to enrich your child's vocabulary and to help them understand the structure of the English language with grammar. Then we'll turn to ELA as a content area as we dive into the study of literature. We'll also talk about the pros and cons of literature-based curricula and how to use them intelligently. Finally, we'll give you some tips on encouraging a love of reading in your child and how to choose literature at the right level for both academic study and recreational reading.

Vocabulary

Have you ever known what a word means but not how to pronounce it? When a word is learned in context, that's a common feeling, and one of the best ways to learn vocabulary. When homeschooling, we can contextualize new vocabulary by showing an example of when the vocabulary is used. "'Accentuate' means to emphasize." Then, ask the students to make the word their own by creating their own sentence. "How else can you use 'accentuate,' Tammy?"

The Common Core English language arts standards recommend instruction in Tier 2 vocabulary words: "words that characterize written and especially academic text—but are not so common in everyday conversation."[1] These words are frequently called "academic vocabulary," and you should make sure that your children study them. We think this emphasis is one of the better sections of the Common Core recommendations.

---

1   Beck, I L McKeown, M G and Kucan, L (2008) *Bringing Words to Life*, Guilford Press.

Explicit instruction is the best way forward. If you choose to go this route, then we suggest obtaining a grade level academic vocabulary list, and teaching one or two words per week, in context. We particularly like the Berkeley Unified School District document and included lists because they include helpful worksheets, teaching suggestions, and links to more information.

High-quality literature, science, and social studies curricula almost always highlight the important domain-specific vocabulary words—what *Bringing Words to Life* calls Tier 3 vocabulary words—for you. You can also choose those words yourself, particularly with literature that your child is studying. As we discussed in chapter 7, a single exposure to the vocabulary word is insufficient for learning the word, so you'll probably need to add more practice to your child's studies.

As you might remember from your own elementary education, simply copying the definition of a word from the glossary or dictionary doesn't force you to remember the meaning. In fact, many of the methods used to teach vocabulary in the past have now been proven to be inadequate by educational researchers. "Do you understand?" is guaranteed to get you cheerful nods of compliance but very few long-term gains in learning the word. Luckily, specifically teaching vocabulary isn't usually difficult.

Simply introduce the word, explaining any roots and suffixes or prefixes. Have the students practice the word in a sentence. Then, have the students use their own words to explain the vocabulary word (elaboration). Often, it's helpful to have students sketch or act out the word. Then, assign some exercises for using the word, and don't forget to quiz them on it later. We recommend either low-tech homemade flashcards or an online flashcard app to help memorize the meanings of those words in a snap.

Then, for next-level learning, give your child more explicit practice by integrating new vocabulary into composition exercises. *The Writing Revolution* has excellent strategies for this and we're particularly fond of the "Because, But, So" technique. In this technique, you'd create three sentence stems with the key vocabulary word and then have your child finish composing the sentences. "Because Lila had cerulean eyes… But the sea around the Greek island was cerulean… So the sky that day was cerulean…" Other curricula also offer strategies for working with vocabulary words, like the *Exploring the World through Story* series by Andrew Campbell (Quidnam Press). If you want to learn more about the why and how of teaching vocabulary, we recommend reading *Bringing Words to Life* (Beck, McKeown, and Lucan, 2002) for yourself.

If you're too busy to create custom vocabulary instruction, or you have a whole slew of children to instruct, or you just don't have an interest in creating your own vocabulary studies program, you're in luck. There are several excellent open-and-go choices for systematically and thoroughly teaching vocabulary. One great choice that will take your student through 12th grade is *Vocabulary for Classical Roots* (Nancy Flowers and Norma Fifer, 1990). This program teaches the Latin and Greek roots that form the basis of much English vocabulary, especially in the sciences. Drew also recommends *Merriam Webster's Vocabulary Builder* by Mary W. Cornog (1994) as a thorough but inexpensive vocabulary book for high school.

Vocabulary Workshop series published by Sadlier is a more traditional program and one of our favorites because the publisher has written and made available many free online resources. When compared to *Vocabulary from Classical Roots*, *Vocabulary Workshop* includes more prepared exercises for the student, requiring less work (and fewer flashcards). However, the teacher's manuals are difficult to obtain for homeschoolers, so the included vocabulary might keep you on your toes.

One way to use these resources is to have each child start a vocabulary notebook that they can add to as time goes on. If you use *Spelling Workout*, you might have your child include the spelling rule they're teaching that week, as well. Likewise, with *Vocabulary from Classical Roots*, you can have your child add the root words and their derivatives. Over the course of a year, in combination with steady retrieval practice, your child will systematically add key words to their vocabulary, raising their reading comprehension ability across subjects.

Grammar

As Hillocks and Smith state in the "Grammar and Usage" chapter in their *Handbook of Research on Teaching the English Language,* "[r]esearch over a period of nearly 90 years has consistently shown that the teaching of school grammar has little or no effect on students." More specifically, learning about English grammar does not appear to result in better student writing.

We still teach it, and we think you should too. Why?

First, understanding grammatical terminology is part of cultural literacy and academic competence. We need to be able to talk to our children about language using standard academic terms. Just as you wouldn't try to teach pre-algebra without using terms like "equation" and "denominator," it's hard to talk about language without referring to "nouns" or "clauses." Students who go on to study a foreign language in middle school or who want to pass a community college placement test will need to know these terms.

In addition, formal grammar instruction helps children understand the structure of language they've been using intuitively all along. That's even more important for English learners and native speakers of dialects other than standard American English—like Courtney. She says, "I come from down a holler, and my everyday English ain't standard." But she can code switch because she has explicitly studied grammar, and so have her children. As Seidenberg and Washington note in their article "Teaching Reading to African American Children" in the Summer 2021 issue of *American Educator,* "simply providing full-form models of classroom language is helpful"[2] and explicit grammar teaching certainly does that.

Finally, we would argue that the purpose of studying grammar is the development of analysis skills, not composition skills. Grammar is about decoding language structures, while composition involves encoding them. Like reading and spelling, they are two sides of the same coin, and we shouldn't ignore either of them.

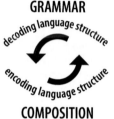

GRAMMAR

decoding language structure

encoding language structure

COMPOSITION

Literature

Literature, as the name of an academic subject, refers to the study of stories, novels, poems, plays, and creative nonfiction like essays or memoirs. Literature study involves reading, analyzing, discussing, and (importantly!) writing about the works students have read. A skilled literature teacher or a high-quality literature program will bring in themes, symbolism, structure, related works, historical context, vocabulary, interpretation, and more. Unless you have serious chops in literary analysis, just handing your child a book and then discussing it with them over dinner is not the same thing, in the same way that sizing up a baking recipe isn't a sufficient lesson in operations with fractions.

Reading vs. Studying Literature

As the previous paragraph suggests, there's a qualitative difference between reading a book and studying one.

Checking for understanding and offering at the very least a high-quality discussion with later retrieval practice is the minimum needed in order to make sure that children understand and retain knowledge. This is one reason we are so adamant about using curriculum created by subject experts.

---

2   Washington, J A and Seidenberg M S (Summer 2021) "Teaching Reading to African American Children: When Home and School Language Differ", *American Educator*, bit.ly/3KUDt3V

Literature-Based Curricula and Literature Studies

It's also the reason we don't recommend most literature-based curricula; the appeal is obvious. Literature-based curriculum companies market their products as the opposite of the public school experience; they eschew textbooks in favor of great literature and deep discussions. But have you ever heard the phrase "a mile wide and an inch deep"? That's how Jenn describes most literature-based curricula.

Reading lists containing upwards of 30 books for a school year make for an impressive transcript. However, if students are only reading those books and not actually studying them, their understanding will remain superficial at best. Students should be studying vocabulary as well as the elements of literature:

- Plot
- Setting
- Characters
- Point of view
- Theme
- Tone

Reading alone doesn't translate into knowledge in the long-term memory. While literature-based curricula do cover literary elements a bit at a time, we don't know of any that includes fact-based memory work, testing or any form of retrieval practice other than narration, often oral.

What we see time and again is that parents using literature-based curricula read (often aloud) with their younger children, but the older kids get handed a book to read independently. The parent has good intentions; independent reading is valuable, as are the discussions that the parent plans to have with the child. But often the parents don't have time to read the book themselves and end up using summaries or notes to guide their discussion—if they get around to it at all. It's not surprising that such discussions are "a mile wide and an inch deep." Literature-based curricula used alone are simply exposure to great stories, *not* a complete education.

Jenn used literature-based programs for years with her children each afternoon. In the mornings, she taught grammar, writing, spelling, vocabulary, science, and history with scripted curricula and textbooks. She then used those themed, literature-based cores to cover electives and to offer broad exposure in social studies. As much as she wanted to be able to order an entire level in a box and be done with it, her kids needed the explicit teaching that textbooks provide. After she tried to make vocabulary and history tests from lit plans one year, she swore off reinventing the wheel. It's hard enough to homeschool when you have everything planned out for you; implementing it all alone is a huge task.

Her compromise was to order one set of books a year and use them with all her kids. She was too busy teaching to pre-read all those books, but they did find some treasures that way. Because she was already teaching the core subjects in an organized, academic way, she wasn't relying on the literature-based curriculum to help her kids make explicit connections between their history class and the historical fiction they read together.

Fans of Charlotte Mason and literature-based curricula may think these critiques are merely theoretical or ideological. We assure you they come from our personal and professional experience. We know middle-aged homeschool graduates who were educated in this style: morning read-alouds of classic literature and poetry; a daily math lesson; uninterrupted reading time of high-quality literature; an emphasis on classical music appreciation; child-led writing in nature journals; and a half-day minimum outside in the natural world. This sounds great to a lot of people, and it works—to an extent. You could get excellent SAT scores this way. We know a homeschooler who was admitted to an Ivy League school with top SAT score, where they promptly bombed out the first semester. They'd never had to write an academic expository essay in history, complete a research paper with footnotes and a bibliography in English, or take a timed final exam in calculus. They hadn't had a formal science lab. They didn't know how to "show their work" in math or seek help from an overburdened TA. This is why good literature is not enough.

How to Use Literature-Based Curricula Wisely

Literature-based curricula often have wonderful book lists, and even if you don't want to rely on the curriculum for your entire homeschooling program, you can easily mine their lists to support another approach. Maybe you want to do a literature-centric American history year. Look and see what popular literature-based programs are using for American history. Those professionals have put the work in for you already. There's no need to discover brand new books. If you're inclined to a favorite book from your own reading or something that looked  good at a bookstore, that works too. There are many resources for you to use.

If your library is open, simply go to the relevant part of the stacks, grab a pile of books, sit down on the floor, and start flipping through them. If you're inclined toward online shopping, you can use Amazon as a search engine. If you already have the title, searching is easy.

If you're creating a new book list for your child's special interest, or middle grade history or science, you may not have many choices. When you keep running into adult books, you might want to add "middle grade" or "YA" to your search term. If that works, then you can sort by "nonfiction" or "historical fiction." For example, your entry in the search bar might look like this: "middle grade" AND "nonfiction" AND "biology."

Reading Levels for Literature Studies and Recreational Reading

Middle grade is a publishing term of art. This refers to books meant to be read by children around ages 9-12. Typically, those are the same books aimed at grades four through six. *Young adult*, usually abbreviated "YA," is used to refer to books aimed at ages 12 and up, which is 7th grade and older. However, as the YA market has become more diverse lately, you'll find that many adults read YA, some almost exclusively YA.

Middle grade titles will often have a main character around age 12. In contrast, YA books often have characters aged 15 to 17. The age gap between main characters and intended ages of readers is deliberate. Typical children like to read about main characters slightly older than themselves.

YA themes are nearly adult. When you read these books, you will find themes and situations that some teenagers may deal with in their day to day lives. These books often have experimentation with drugs and alcohol on the page, not just referenced in an aside. Another distinctive feature of YA books is that main characters explore their sexuality, sometimes explicitly.

When you make your book list, ensure you are making wise choices about your book selections. Just because your child is testing at the high school level for vocabulary does not mean that your child is emotionally or intellectually ready to read YA books. Choosing books that suit your child's social emotional development is just as important as choosing books that support their intellectual development. Sometimes, depending on how advanced your child is at reading, finding the right book for your child can be a tricky balance.

Another consideration for your book list is the ratio of fiction to nonfiction, typically suggested at a 60:40 split. If your child prefers to read nonfiction, then tip the sixty percent to nonfiction. The professional recommendation is for nonfiction written at or just under the reading level of your child. That doesn't mean a board book for your 8-year-old. It does mean that your high schooler shouldn't have to struggle with a dictionary to get through a college level text.

You need to ensure that the fiction to nonfiction ratio is balanced. The purpose of having your child read a variety of books in a particular subject is to provide them with different perspectives. Nonfiction provides a valuable point of view, particularly nonfiction from the time period under study.

Pros and Cons of Historical Fiction

Historical fiction set in the time period you're studying can provide fascinating insight into the lives of everyday people, or what historians call social history. Historical fiction makes history come alive. Historians tell what happened and why and why it matters, but a good historical novel will show you what it felt like to be there. Jenn is a big proponent of textbook learning, but let's admit it, not all history texts make for compelling reading. In Jenn's opinion, historical fiction provides balance, making it the other half of a good history class.

It's one thing to say that the United States was divided during the Civil War. States on the border often had family members fighting for both sides. Knowing the dates of the battles is important, but so is imagining what it felt like to have your father fight for the North while your brothers fought for the South. Experiencing historical events in first person is often not just the gateway to becoming an amateur historian but also an empathetic human.

Historical fiction isn't just a prettier, more deluxe version of real events. The insights students get from historical fiction can help them make sense of contemporary issues—and even provide a peek into future possibilities. As we know, history tends to repeat itself. In historical fiction, those tragic events have already occurred, and we can learn from the past without waiting for history to repeat itself again and again. Historical fiction shows us that human nature doesn't change that much but how we treat others can. Jenn is very much in favor of it for these reasons.

Courtney, however, is leerier of historical fiction. When choosing historical fiction, you want to be aware of *chronotopes*,[3] or the idea that the setting in a book, particularly in historical fiction, is secondary to the goals of the author in the story. For example, there were simply not enough British dukes to make

---

3   This term was coined by Russian literary scholar Mikhail Bakhtin in 1937.

good stories for the romance novel market.[4] If you based your understanding of the Regency era solely on romance novels, you'd come away with a seriously skewed vision of the period. This may seem like a minor problem, but uncritically using historical fiction in education can significantly change the way our children see the world.

No author is perfectly neutral in their portrayal of history. The beloved *Little House on the Prairie* series is notorious not only for its negative portrayal of Native Americans, but also for being edited to promote a libertarian perspective.[5] It's simply not possible for authors to separate themselves from  the story they're telling; they are responsible for choosing what to leave in and what to leave out.[6] One famous literary example of the power of what is left out is Shirley Jackon's "The Lottery." Not until the very end of the story do we realize that Jackson isn't talking about Powerball! What is left out of *Little House on the Prairie*? Where is the Native American perspective on Laura's family or the information about Laura's sister happily attending a state-funded school for the Deaf and blind?

In some cases, the problem with historical fiction lies not in what is excluded but in the bias of what is included. One popular literature-based curriculum for homeschoolers uses *The Clan of the Cave Bear* as a window into Neanderthal life and culture. The problem is that Jean M. Auel used a thinly disguised version of 1970s culture as the basis for her book[7] and anthropology has moved on in the last 40 years.[8] Students who read the book will reasonably assume that it's telling the truth when it repeats repugnant old ideas, like the notion that "the Neanderthal's skull alone was proof of its darkness and stupidity." Or, "[t]he thoughts and desires which once dwelt within it never soared beyond those of a brute…"[9] There is straight eugenicist line between the 1920s anthropological ideas about Neanderthals as dark, stupid, and brutish, and the Nazi call for

4   *History Ever After, Part I: The Fabricated Chronotope*, Jennifer Hallock, bit.ly/3CaArpG

5   Woodside, C (2016) "How 'Little House on the Prairie' Built Modern Conservatism", *Politico Magazine*, politi.co/3c23Mbk

6   Sugiyama, M S (1996) "On the origins of narrative: Storyteller bias as a fitness-enhancing strategy," *Human Nature*, 7(4) 403-425.

7   Cengage Learning Gale (2017) *A Study Guide for Jean M. Auel's The Clan of the Cave Bear*, Gale Study Guides.

8   Curry, A (2010) "Fate of the Cave Bear", *Smithsonian* Magazine, bit.ly/3T0kpof

9   Mooallem, J (2017) "Neanderthals Were People, Too," 11 January, *The New York Times*.

killing those with disabilities. Using this book as an educational tool is not, therefore, a good choice.

In addition, most authors want people to enjoy their stories, so they omit uncomfortable details or change the perspective to avoid making the majority of readers dislike the story. For example, *The Boy in the Striped Pyjamas* has been held out as an example of what not to teach by the Centre for Holocaust Education at University College London because it changes the perspective from those who were killed, the Jews, to the Germans, who were doing the killing. In this way, the book creates sympathy for Nazis, as borne out by research studying children who were taught the book in their literature classes. Teaching children history through fiction muddies the waters about what was real and what wasn't. The research shows that many children who were taught the book saw it as a truthful example of history and believed that ordinary Germans were unaware of the Holocaust.[10] This happened despite the fact that the book's subtitle is *"A Fable."*

Whether or not you choose to use historical fiction, or how, is up to you. If you do use it, we recommend it as a supplement to a neutral, fact-based narrative history (like a good textbook), not as the main source of historical information. Choose carefully, with an eye to historical accuracy as well as literary merit, and be prepared to discuss any questionable perspectives with your child to make sure they're coming away with a balanced and realistic view of the historical issues.

---

10 Sherwood, H (2022) "The Boy in the Striped Pyjamas 'may fuel dangerous Holocaust fallacies,'" 27 January, *The Guardian*.

CHAPTER 11

NOTES ON MATH

Math education in the US has been fraught for decades. Those of us who attended public schools in the 1970s and '80s remember being subjected to an ever-changing array of teaching methods in what has become known in education circles as "the Math Wars." Millennials may have lingering anxiety from the high-stakes testing they were subjected to in school. Unless you have a strong STEM background, you might be worried about your ability to teach this subject. In this chapter, we'll take you through some definitions and ideas that will help you make sense of the controversies surrounding math pedagogy and, we hope, increase your confidence with teaching math in your homeschool, even if you feel your own education in mathematics was poor.

Conceptual vs. Procedural

In math, there are several lines of conflict. For example, how would you feel about a math lesson that consisted of presenting a difficult math task and having your children work to solve it? Their final product would be a poster to demonstrate their understanding. Keep in mind that your child would not be given background information. They would not be given explicit instructions on how to solve the problem. They would not be given a rubric for success. They would not be required to demonstrate that they could solve a set of problems that used the concepts.

Does this sound absurd to you? This sequence is the model lesson shared by the National Council for the Teachers of Mathematics, in "What Do the Standards for Mathematical Practice Mean to You?" (Rutherford, 2015). You might think that this situation is frustrating for students, to be given a task and no instruction in how to solve the task, and you'd be right. Students at Green Hope High School in Cary, North Carolina, were so frustrated that they staged a walkout in protest of this kind of curriculum. Parents were public in their disapproval, so the organization that created the curriculum sued. A parent filed a countersuit, which led to the dismissal of the original lawsuit. (Drew withdrew their daughter from a public charter school in 9th grade over this kind of teaching.)

Most math curricula emphasize procedures or concepts, but not both. While we appreciate conceptual understanding, like the North Carolina parents, what we're regularly concerned with is, "Can my children do math, efficiently and on grade level?" In our opinion, procedural emphasis curricula ensure that math gets done right, and they are our first choice. Conceptual understanding is important, but most children cannot develop conceptual understanding in a vacuum.

Conceptual-emphasis curricula also raise equity issues. When we teach our children with special education needs, fluency is a major goal. Students with working memory issues are helped by curricula that emphasize memorization of basic facts and procedures. Many students don't have the luxury of good working memory to re-derive procedures or good executive functioning to focus through lengthy procedures. They need to be able to just do it by combining memorized chunks of processes in limited working memory.

A curriculum that promises to deepen conceptual understanding by teaching through critical thinking or problem solving is not suitable for most children. Working to frustration level every day isn't sustainable for long-term progress. Instead, choose a curriculum with a manageable amount of work, with sufficient repetitions to cement understanding and at a high enough intensity to keep your child focused on the topic.

Don't fall for the line that children need conceptual understanding because otherwise they're just memorizing and regurgitating. Remember that facts are required to build the mental architecture of your child's mind. Conceptual-first is no more a valid argument than that of nature versus nurture. You need *both*, and you develop conceptual understanding by working with facts that you know.

Natural Math vs. Direct Instruction

Natural math sounds very appealing. Who doesn't like things that are natural? Seeing math in everyday life sounds excellent, especially if you're a mathematician who does work with patterns. Extending children's knowledge of math by playing games is lovely. However, there are some problems with this.

First, children are not miniature mathematicians. Their brains are functionally different from an adult's. Remember, their working memory differs from an adult, their prefrontal cortexes are immature, and their synaptic learning is higher than an adult's. Their underlying schemas are different. An expert in a field will automatically recognize deep connections, while a child's understanding is more inflexible and shallower.

Second, playing games or baking cookies will only get you so far. Playing games is excellent for reinforcing skills and we know of several curricula that use games in this way. However, games do not *teach* children those skills. "The theory is that concepts are best learned when they are presented in gradually increasing complexity. The reality, Schmidt finds, is that topics are repeated at the same low level."[1]

In addition, the US math curriculum is famously "a mile wide and an inch deep."[2] Games are simply not going to cover the multitude of knowledge, skills, and abilities required in elementary math curricula, much less middle and high school level mathematics. Teaching math with direct instruction has been shown to be the best instruction method, with over 50 years of research to support this conclusion.[3] Saxon math is a direct instruction curriculum.[4]

Also, loitering through math with games, drawing, and cooking is deeply unsystematic. Courtney blames trickle down from the NCTM standards. When "the standards suggest the use of 'math manipulatives,' technology, group work and other strategies...teachers had in fact adopted the teaching strategies but ignored the mathematics...Instead of computing without understanding concepts, students were engaged in hands-on activities without understanding concepts."[5] We see this ignorance of mathematics all the time, and in fact, what little research analysis there is on homeschooled children's mathematics achievement shows that their math achievement is consistently *below* predicted levels.[6]

---

1   Duffrin, E (2005) "Math teaching in U.S. 'inch deep, mile wide'", July 26, *Chicago Reporter*.

2   Schmidt, W H, McKnight, C C and Raizen, S A (1997) "Splintered Vision: An Investigation of U.S. Mathematics and Science Education, Executive Summary", U.S. National Research Center for the Third International Mathematics and Science Study.

3   Stockard, J, Wood, T W, Coughlin, C and Khoury, C R (2018) "The Effectiveness of Direct Instruction Curricula: A Meta-Analysis of a Half Century of Research", *Review of Educational Research* 88(4) 479-507.

4   *Five Meanings of Direct Instruction* by Barak Rosenshine, 2008, Academic Development Institute.

5   Duffrin (2005).

6   Kunzman, R and Gaither, M (2013) "Homeschooling: A Comprehensive Survey of the Research", *Other Education: The Journal of Educational Alternatives* 2(1) 4-59.

Finally, many people who claim to be doing "natural math" studies are simply not doing any math at all. Again, we frequently see this in our roles as homeschool consultants and end-of-year homeschool assessors. Just this week, Courtney met with a parent who did "everyday math," by which the parent meant no math instruction at all. We also know of this lack of instruction from others who provide math tutoring to homeschoolers or work with homeschoolers in other capacities.

Note: By "everyday math," we aren't referring to the once-widespread *Everyday Math* curriculum, which was famously reviled among math teachers. One headline: "Is Everyday Math The Worst Math Program Ever?" (Emily Willingham in *Forbes*, 2013).

Interleaved, Interval-Spaced Retrieval Practice

To be most effective, practice should be (1) spaced, (2) interleaved, and (3) varied.

What does this mean when choosing a homeschool math curriculum? One of the key debates is whether to teach for mastery. In mastery-based teaching, each concept is taught only once, but thoroughly; students are not taught the concept again. For example, Math-U-See is a unique homeschool math curriculum that does not follow the typical math instruction schedule. Instead, it focuses on one topic at a time. Many handwriting instruction programs are similar because students use their handwriting across the curriculum. This is in opposition to spiral curriculum, the other side of the debate, when concepts are reviewed throughout the year and more depth of knowledge is added at each visit. Saxon Math is an example of this type of program, with problem sets that typically contain about 20% new material (from that day's instruction) and 80% old material, from previous weeks and months. Many world language programs intermix new and old material as well.

The merits of each type are debated, but given that cognitive science supports interleaved, interval-spaced retrieval practice, a spiral design benefits most students. We choose a spiral curriculum whenever possible. This means "a spiraling series of exercises that cycle back to key skill sets in a seemingly random sequence that adds layers of context and meaning at each turn" (*Make It Stick*, 2014, 50).

Many US curricula combine the worst parts of mastery and spiral curriculum. For example, most math textbooks have a chapter on fractions. Students learn one type of fraction per lesson, take a chapter test, and don't learn about fractions again until the next year. While technically this is a spiral, this is not a useful spiral—instead, as Willingham (2012) writes in *When Can You Trust the Experts: How to Tell Good Science from Bad in Education*, "students don't stick with any topic long enough to develop a deep conceptual understanding."

In poor curricula:

- practice is not spaced—students have only one or two days to learn the information and practice the knowledge, skills, or abilities taught.

- practice isn't interleaved—For example, the homework might have 10 problems of type 1, 10 of type 2, and 10 of type 3, in that order.

- practice is not varied—homework is only on that day's concepts or procedures.

Parents and children tend to dislike intensive spiral curricula because spacing out practice means that children have to put forth more effort to remember. Interleaved practice feels more difficult than massed practice because it seems hard, chaotic, or boring. Varied practice loses the sense of mastery students get from successfully completing ten problems in a row. And that makes children cranky, which leads to whining, we know. We still recommend that you choose a curriculum with built-in interleaved, interval-spaced retrieval practice whenever possible.

When Jenn thinks about spaced retrieval practice, Saxon Math immediately comes to mind. A few of her children had a hate/tolerate relationship with it. This is where Jenn will lean on her experience and tell you that kids don't have to love or even like their materials. Sometimes they do, and that's cool. But since you are the adult in charge, you must insist that the work be done. Jenn jumped around to different curricula too many times thinking that if her child liked the new curriculum, they would work harder (or at least with fewer complaints). The problem was not the curriculum; the problem was the effort required to learn math.

Anyone who thinks that their kids are not capable of memorizing huge swaths of material need look no farther than Pokémon, Minecraft formulas, and whatever their special interest contains. Courtney's oldest daughter had terrible difficulty with her math facts, but she could memorize how to pronounce every single dinosaur in the Carnegie Natural History Museum. If she could do that, she could memorize her math facts—and she did, eventually.

Real learning is usually not easy—and "learning to learn" is worth your time. Knowing how to buckle down and get it done is a great life skill. Gaining the skills required to work through difficult concepts, rehearse for performance, and then demonstrate expertise is preparing for adulthood.

People are capable of great things, but your children don't have to already be great in elementary school. Take the time to go slow and lay firm foundations for the rest of their mental architecture. Later teachers will thank you (or maybe you'll thank yourself) for embedding place value and the underlying concepts of the distributive property in early elementary school.

CHAPTER 12

NOTES ON SOCIAL STUDIES

In this chapter, we'll focus on the areas within social studies that are commonly taught in K–12 schools: geography, history, and civics. Taken more broadly, social studies can include the social sciences such as anthropology and sociology, but these are usually reserved for college-level study, so we won't be discussing them here. A simple introduction to economics is commonly taught in elementary school, and the subject may form a stand-alone high school course—in New York State, it's offered in 12th grade. Finally, we'll also talk about the importance of religious literacy—learning *about* religions in a neutral, secular way—as part of social studies.

Geography

While those only familiar with the US education system might find it surprising, other countries, such as the UK, treat geography as a separate subject with its own disciplinary knowledge. One of the advantages of homeschooling is that you, too, can make geography a separate subject. For example, Courtney has consistently used Evan-Moor's *Daily Geography* program with her  elementary-age children. As children age out of such programs, you might choose to integrate geography into the history curriculum or spend a year with world geography as an emphasis, as is common in US middle schools.

One of the common confusions about geography is that it is strictly map work. Yes, learning how to read maps is an important part of geography, but geography as a discipline is about more than physical geography. Volcanoes exist, rivers exist, mountains exist, and those tend to be inherently less controversial than the other parts of geography.

However, the other half of geography, and arguably the main focus of the discipline in higher education, is what is known as human geography, or how humans interact with their environment. This includes the countries of the world, as well as the religious beliefs, ways in which people group themselves within countries, and often facts about those people, such as the languages they speak (which can lead to uncomfortable discussions about history), literacy rates (often directly related to governments' spending choices, which then lead to discussions about economics), common employment (countries with coasts tend to have fishing fleets and eat fish, for example), and so on. In our homeschools, we can go into depth and breadth, balancing both physical and human geography.

History

After science, history is probably the most politically contested subject in the K–12 curriculum. We encourage homeschoolers to take a balanced approach to history that includes both factual narratives and the voices of those marginalized by the mainstream. Historical arguments change over time and designing your homeschool only in response to the concerns of the day risks doing your children a disservice by not providing them with underlying knowledge to make sense of those issues.

For example, Courtney picked up *A Different Mirror for Young People: A History of Multicultural America*, which is described on the cover copy as a book that "brings ethnic history alive." This is certainly a valuable addition to homeschool studies, but it's explicitly written as a challenge to what the author, Ronald Takaki, calls the "Master Narrative." In the beginning of the book, Takaki describes it as an effort to "recover the missing chapters of American history." This is not a retelling of the traditional story, and Takaki is explicit that telling the story is not his goal.

In fact, Takaki assumes that students have already been exposed to the Master Narrative—but in our experience, many have not. Drew's daughter attended a public elementary school in Massachusetts for a year and half, from the middle of 5th grade through 6th, and in that time, she did not receive any instruction in history. Only at the public charter she attended for middle school and upper high school was history consistently taught, and even then, the instruction was more often topical than narrative, designed to fulfill the letter of the law as it applied to the state's standards. As a result, very few, if any, students graduated with a clear understanding of historical actors and events, let alone with the ability to form and present cogent analyses of causes and effects in history. In Courtney's excellent local school district (consistently ranked second or third in the state), students do not have dedicated history and science classes until sixth grade. These 7th graders might not know the difference between a state and a country. They might not know the seven seas, or the continents, much less where countries are on continents. England, to them, might be best known as the home of a soccer team, and possibly where their language came from.

So, Courtney thinks that, in order for our children to understand the history shared in this perspective, we should also teach them an integrated strand of narrative history. For example, Takaki introduces the Jamestown settlement as, "English colonists settled in Virginia in 1607 and Massachusetts in 1620." There are no maps and very little backstory. Social studies teachers across the country would probably agree that many average 7th-graders might not know where England, Massachusetts, or Virginia are. They almost certainly couldn't locate Jamestown on a map. In addition, there is no discussion of daily life at the colony, and no  mention of women and children in the colony. Instead, Takaki begins with, "At the Jamestown colony in Virginia, the English found themselves living in the ancestral homeland of about fourteen thousand Powhatan Indians" (31). Did aliens dump the colonists there? Why does Takaki call them colonizers? What are colonizers, anyway? Colonists are never explicitly defined in that chapter.

Without the backstory provided by other, more traditional, texts, the stories shared in these kinds of books are isolated tales scattered through history. However, if we make an effort to weave this knowledge into the wider tapestry of history, allowing our children to see how our history can have more than one perspective, we do a better job of preparing them for adulthood and participation in the civic life of our country. Arguably, one of the markers of adulthood is being able to hold the cognitive dissonance of knowing that two reasonable people, given the same information and issues, can disagree on the path forward.

Choosing History Spines

A spine is a text that teachers refer back to and expand on throughout the school year. Much like a spine holds the body together, a spine text is the organizing structure of a course. While not all spines are textbooks, all textbooks are spines. One of the joys of homeschooling is finding good books to be the spine for your child's studies, allowing for "rabbit trails" or deep dives into side subjects mentioned in the spine.

As we saw in the chapter on teaching literature, historical fiction does not make a good spine. Fiction, by its very nature, tells a story, and so the emphasis in fiction is on the story, rather than the information. Unreliable narrators, time skips, the use of chronotopes, and other literary devices make systematic exploration of content difficult. Instead, choose a nonfiction survey or an age-appropriate textbook as your spine. This will provide clear structure and a good foundation for further study.

When choosing a spine, take care to use a text that is both respectful and inclusive of other cultures. We routinely see curricula that use texts that are out of copyright as spines, but those older texts are out of print for a reason. For example, *The Story of Mankind* by Hendrick Van Loon is regularly recommended as a world history text for the younger set because it's free on Gutenberg and similar sites, but we believe it is a poor choice for 21st-century families.

To see why, let's examine an excerpt from *The Story of Mankind*. Specifically, we can look at how the text treats Mohammed. This section of the text begins with,

> In the seventh century, another Semitic tribe appeared upon the scene and challenged the power of the west. They were the Arabs, peaceful shepherds who had roamed through the deserts since the beginning of time without showing any signs of imperial ambitions.

There is so much wrong with this and on so many levels that it's hard to know where to start. If we do nothing more than look up "Arabs" in Wikipedia (acknowledging that Wikipedia itself is hardly a perfect source), we see "The Nabateans, an Arab people, formed their kingdom near Petra in the 3rd century BC. Arab tribes, most notably, the Ghassanids and the Lakhmids, began to appear in the southern Syrian Desert from the mid 3rd century onward, during the mid to later stages of the Roman and Sasanian empires." Obviously, these are not people without imperial ambitions.

When we talk about religious figures with our children, we try to treat them with the respect that they deserve. For an example of disrespect from *The Story of Mankind*, Van Loon doesn't actually call the prophet of Islam by the name Mohammed. Instead, Van Loon calls him "Ahmed, the camel driver who became the prophet of the Arabian desert." In another instance of disrespect, you would not go up to a Christian and start talking about how Jesus was not really divinely inspired. But, Van Loon says that Mohammed was an epileptic, that he wasn't divinely inspired. Instead, Van Loon writes that Mohammed was suffering from spells of unconsciousness. This is a shocking perspective on a non-Christian religion. We find this treatment of religious figures and cultures to be a pressing reason not to base a curriculum around old texts.

Other Content Concerns

It's not just the treatment of non-European cultures or non-Christian faiths that can be problematic in social studies texts. Curriculum from religious publishers often contain interpretations that one might find concerning. For example, you might see a civics textbook that begins with, "All governments are ordained by God, but none compare to government by God, theocracy" (*American Government in Christian Perspective*, Abeka). On the matter of race, these kinds of textbooks include statements like "Indians' worship of false gods kept them from advancing the way the Europeans had" (*The History of the United States*, Abeka). Statements about apartheid include: "Since 'the power to tax is the power to destroy,' white South Africans attempted to create a system that would protect their interests from a nontaxpaying majority" (*Social Studies 1086*, ACE). Statements about slavery include: "Growth of the Slave Trade... Europeans were unable to survive heavy work in the hot, tropical climate. To many people, Africans seemed the best solution, for they came from a similar climate where they were used to doing hard work" (*Heritage Studies*, BJU Press).

Homeschoolers should be aware of the bias in social studies texts and choose materials that align with their educational priorities.

Civics

Like history, civics is subject to pedagogical debates. One of the oldest splits in teaching civics is whether the primary goal should be to encourage children to love their country or to critique its shortcomings. The former approach aims to create what E. D. Hirsch, Jr. calls "loyal citizens of the republic" (*How to Educate a Citizen*, 2021), in a long-term investment for the health of our government. On the other side of the divide is the view that, as Nikole Hannah-Jones wrote in *The 1619 Project* (2019), "[o]ur democracy's founding ideals were false when they were written. Black Americans have fought to make them true". This may seem like a modern debate, but despite the latest tempest in the social media teapot, arguments about how and what to teach our children about our country have been going on almost since the US was founded.

For example, as Timothy Egan wrote in the *New York Times* in 2001, "The era of Catholic schools in America dates to 1884, when the bishops, responding to complaints about Protestant domination of public schools, ordered every parish to build a school. Waves of mostly poor, immigrant children were educated at these schools, which engendered a backlash." Even then, public schools explicitly taught children to become "American," which meant Protestant. Still today, Courtney regularly meets people who view Catholics as pagans. Famously, President Grant wanted public schools, "unmixed with atheistic, pagan or sectarian teaching" (*Ulysses S. Grant, Politician*, Hesseltine, 1935). While, theoretically, the debate has moved on from which religion should be promoted in public schools, the argument about what makes a true American citizen remains.

Knowing our current laws and standards for citizenship helps prepare our children to engage as adult citizens of the USA. As homeschoolers, we can teach our children what being a citizen of the USA entails. For example, former Supreme Court Justice Sandra Day O'Connor founded iCivics in 2009, explicitly to teach children about our system of government. Available as a free resource, it's a middle of the road option to teach children about their adult responsibilities and obligations as citizens.

Religious Literacy

Religious studies are an often-neglected part of social studies that we believe needs greater emphasis. We're not talking about religious education here—inculcating the beliefs of a particular faith—but about learning about various religious beliefs and communities as part of cultural literacy. In the United States, at least, this area of social studies is neglected by both secular and religious homeschoolers alike, albeit for different reasons.

Many US-based homeschoolers might not be aware that the National Council for the Social Studies (NCSS), the lead organization for guiding how social studies is taught in the USA, has as official policy that children in the USA should be taught about religion, both from a historical perspective and from a comparative studies point of view. There are six key attributes for this study, based on Panoch's 1974 guidelines and adopted by the First Amendment Center. As per the NCSS and the American Academy of Religion (AAR), those attributes are:

- study should be academic, not devotional
- study should be for awareness, not acceptance
- study should be about religion, not the practice of a religion
- study should expose children to a religion, not impose a view
- study should educate, not promote or denigrate
- study should inform, not press children to conform

The AAR has identified three main prongs of understanding: the basic tenets of religious traditions, the diversity of expressions and beliefs in those traditions, and the major role that religion plays in society, both historically and today. In their 2010 "Guidelines for Teaching about Religion," they have identified four main instructional approaches:

- the historical approach
- the literary approach
- the traditions based approach
- the cultural studies approach

Each of these is possible in your homeschool. If you belong to a faith tradition, you will likely want to provide *religious education* in that faith as a separate and ongoing thread of your child's education. In the US, many communities have religious education readily available through Sunday school, Hebrew school, and so on. Religious education differs from religious literacy because religious education inculcates your child in your family and community's faith traditions. *Religious literacy* is an academic goal in service of being a better US citizen, not a faith-based goal.

The book *Overcoming Religious Illiteracy* (2007) by Harvard Professor Diane L. Moore presents a theoretical approach for introducing religious studies. Moore believes that we should educate students to be "religiously literate." She goes on to say that if we are more religiously literate, then we are more capable of acting as respectful and intelligent citizens in an increasingly pluralistic society. Generally speaking, she makes a case for the cultural studies approach to overcoming this American educational defect, saying:

> I believe that the purpose of mandatory K–8 or K–12 education in the United States should be for students to acquire the skills and experiences that will enable them 1) to function as active citizens who promote the ideals of democracy; 2) to act as thoughtful and informed moral agents; and 3) to lead fulfilling lives. These three goals are not discrete. Indeed, I will argue throughout this text that they are interrelated and even interdependent. (Moore, 2007)

Even if you are firmly agnostic, we recommend that you obtain and teach with materials that reflect your worldview, so your children are part of your community. Atheists should be familiar with the major world religions because having that knowledge provides modern cultural literacy. Because knowledge of religion is assumed by many, if not most, authors, reading comprehension can depend on religious literacy. Likewise, people of faith should understand the history and viewpoints represented by atheism, agnosticism, and humanism.

Other countries have separate courses in religious literacy. The UK has a particularly nice model for this. For example, the Cambridgeshire Standing Advisory Council on Religious Education (SACRE) has a 68-page "Agreed Syllabus" with detailed progression documents based on age bands (Key Stages) and covered religions (Buddhism, Christianity, Hinduism, Humanism, Islam, Judaism, and Sikhism).

Religious literacy can be studied in the home. For example, Jenn's family does a year of religious studies in grade school, another in middle school, and a semester in high school. Your children might also be reading mythology from around the world. Religious literacy can be gained by teaching about religions during history studies as well as through the study of literature. (The elementary levels of Drew's world literature curriculum, *Exploring the World through Story*, teach religious literacy this way.)

CHAPTER 13
NOTES ON SCIENCE

Like social studies, the teaching of science has become highly politicized in the United States. As secular homeschoolers, we are firmly on the side of teaching the established scientific consensus, not sectarian religious beliefs. However, the homeschooling world is diverse, so parents need to be careful as they choose science curriculum. We'll delve into that topic and offer other suggestions about teaching this subject in this chapter.

Nature Studies

Nature studies might seem foreign to someone coming from a public school environment, but it is an old idea. In 1904, Liberty Hyde Bailey was one of the key figures in founding the extension system. All universities engage in research and teaching, but the nation's more than 100 land-grant colleges and universities have a third, critical mission. Through the nationwide extension service, land-grant colleges and universities fulfill their additional mandate to translate their research into a form usable by agricultural producers, small business owners, consumers, families, and young people.

Bailey was also a wildly popular author. He sold over a million copies of sixty-five books, and edited more than a hundred other books, not to mention thirteen hundred articles and one hundred papers. As part of the extension system's work with land-grant colleges, Bailey was indirectly responsible for 4-H, a network of youth organizations focused on experiential learning in the natural world and administered through the Cooperative Extension system. With half a million volunteers and 3,500 professionals, 4-H works with six million children across the country. Bailey wrote that the purpose of nature was to informally "educate the child in terms of his environment."

In another example, in 1911, Anna Comstock, the first female professor at Cornell University, wrote the acclaimed *Handbook of Nature Study*. Over 100 years later, the book is now in its 24th edition. She wrote and implemented nature study curricula for the public schools. From her perspective, children should learn about the natural world closest to them and then expand their field of studies elsewhere. While nature educators rightly point out that Comstock's work does not adhere to modern conservation ethics, her book remains popular with homeschoolers, especially those who use the Charlotte Mason method.

Why should we listen to these people who wrote over 100 years ago? Here's an idea: shifting baseline syndrome, first identified by Pauly in 1995. When we were children, lightning bugs were so common that in less than five minutes we could put enough in a jar to read by. For our children, they're rare, pretty speckles in the night. For their children, finding a lightning bug might be cause for celebration. What we consider to be a "normal" environment could be considered a degraded environment by a past generation. The baseline has shifted. How does that work? Well, in colonial times, lobsters were considered disgusting poverty food because they were so plentiful. At Courtney's grocery store, they're $20 per pound. Our increased tolerance of a poor environment makes conservation efforts harder because we don't perceive a problem. Of course, lobsters are expensive, right?

While families could make nature study an informal, casual experience through weekly hikes, they could also make nature study the cornerstone of their children's earliest exposure to science. Forest schools have a similar philosophy, but you don't need to enroll your young children in formal education to reap the benefits. Even older children can learn about biodiversity, foodways, and intensive agriculture through local nature study. What foods grow wild in your area? What crops are harvested in your area? How do foods come to be on your table? These are all worth studying.

Issues in Homeschool Science Curricula

Note that homeschoolers need to discern the perspective of any given science curriculum: mainstream (what the rest of the world just calls "science"), neutral (which is still often a religious perspective because it side-steps scientific consensus or places it on par with sectarian beliefs), or openly religious (often but not always Young Earth or anti-macro-evolution).

When thinking about using religious science curricula, one key to understanding is the idea of Young Earth Creationism (YEC), which views the Bible as the literal word of God and interprets the book of Genesis as showing that the Earth and all the life on it were created by God between 6,000 and 10,000 years ago. Therefore, mainstream understanding of geologic history, that the Earth is 4.5 billion years old, is unlikely to be explained in YEC curricula. For example, "God designed the glaciers to store water in the coldest months when water is not usually scarce and to release it in warmer months when streams and reservoirs are low" (*Science*, BJU Press). Similarly, the age of the universe, about 14 billion years, is not often taught in this kind of curriculum. When religious textbooks espouse YEC beliefs, they rarely teach the science of evolution. An elementary science book might claim "... dinosaurs lived on earth at the same time as people did" (*Exploring Creation with Zoology*, Apologia). Some textbooks are more subtle and simply omit the science of evolution.

Sometimes, these curricula are less challenging because rather than explaining the underlying, sometimes counterintuitive, scientific theories, they'll use an explanation such as "because of Jesus." That was an actual line in an old Christian homeschool science book gifted to Jenn's family. It's now one of her family's catch phrases for anything unexplainable. Multiple studies have found that many of these texts are less rigorous than standard textbooks. In a review conducted by the *Orlando Sentinel*, Cynthia Bayer, a biology lecturer at the University of Central Florida, was quoted as saying: "Students who have learned science in this kind of environment are not prepared for college experiences...They would be intellectually disadvantaged."

The "Science Wars"? Science Pedagogy

Aside from the issues with content in religious curricula, there are deep divisions among those who teach science about the best way to teach it, particularly in the earlier years. As discussed in the Scope and Sequence section, the current fashion for elementary science instruction is for *inquiry-based instruction*, having students to design their own "investigations." The current national standards, the *Next Generation Science Standards* rely heavily on inquiry-based instruction.

Courtney finds this emphasis to be patently absurd, as PhDs in science, which are explicitly designed for adults to learn how to conduct scientific investigations, take five to seven years to complete. Your average 7-year-old is not capable of designing a scientific investigation without an adult directing the activity. In other words, the adult provides the equivalent of a worksheet for them to fill out, to ensure that the child has touched on all the key pieces of asking and answering a question. This is hardly a child designing an investigation, and we do our children no favors by pretending otherwise.

One popular alternative is to provide *demonstrations* for your child. We might perform a tricky lab experiment ourselves, having children take notes as we go. Particularly in the elementary years, most science concepts can be demonstrated with materials from around the house. Often, we call this "kitchen table science." Teaching about acids and bases through vinegar and baking soda is a classic example, particularly when paired with pH strips. Preparing slides of onion and pond water is a slightly more complicated than the average kitchen table demonstration, but still well within the money and time budgets of many homeschooling families. Taking advantage of demonstration opportunities in the wider world can also be helpful. In 2017, many families seized the opportunity to show a solar eclipse to their children.

All of these are useful, hands-on learning opportunities that allow adults to introduce difficult concepts and ideas. Embedded in a rigorous, *direct instruction* curriculum that complements the demonstrations with background knowledge, shows children how to interpret the demonstration as it progresses, reviews the key parts of the demonstration in high-quality read-alouds and other texts, and follows up on the demonstration with careful checks for understanding, demonstrations can provide excellent science learning.

However, not all science concepts are easily demonstrated. Without scanning electron microscopes, epithelial cells in bronchial tubes are difficult to show. Even when a visual component is available, it may be difficult to implement. For example, most of us do not have dual vacuum tubes available to demonstrate the force of gravity when friction is absent. Therefore, teaching science often means relying heavily on images or videos of the concept under discussion. Parents can spend a considerable amount of time tracking down materials, images, and videos for teaching purposes. This is where a high-quality curriculum comes into play—all that work is done for you.

CHAPTER 14

NOTES ON WORLD LANGUAGES

The United States lags behind many other countries in foreign language instruction. As of 2017, only 11 US states had foreign language requirements for high school graduation, with an additional 24 treating foreign languages as electives counting toward a diploma. With numbers like that in high school, it's not surprising that relatively few American children study a foreign language in elementary or middle school. Be that as it may, we highly recommend the study of world languages to homeschoolers.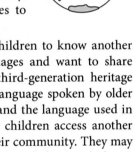

Families have many practical reasons for wanting children to know another language. The parents might speak different languages and want to share those with their kids. They might be second- or third-generation heritage speakers who want to pass on their culture via the language spoken by older relatives. They might want their children to understand the language used in their faith tradition. They might want to help their children access another culture's literature or make friends with people in their community. They may be living abroad and have easy access to native speakers, or they might know of an excellent language teacher in their area. Or the child might ask to learn a language because of a hobby or interest; in recent years, Gen Z has gravitated toward Japanese and Korean, probably due to the popularity of anime, Vtubers, and K-Pop.

As US citizens, we think Spanish is an important language for our children to learn. More than one in ten US residents speak Spanish at home. Another 12 million US residents are bilingual in Spanish. Worldwide, the US is home to the second largest population of Spanish speakers. Despite six years of Latin, Courtney's eldest has decided that Spanish will be her high school language study because she thinks it will be more useful. Courtney agrees with her and is supporting her in that decision. So, although foreign language study is optional in grades K–8, we urge you to consider it. Younger students should focus on building vocabulary and basic language structures through immersion in the spoken language. Yes, that's true even with classical languages like Latin or Greek.

Unless you're fluent or can find a scripted program for the target language, you're likely going to want to outsource foreign language instruction. Look for teachers who show familiarity with modern research on language acquisition and how that translates into sound, age-appropriate pedagogy. If a class consists of little more than grammar drills and vocabulary worksheets, with few opportunities for students to use the language for authentic communication, look elsewhere. You want to see phrases like "communicative approach" and "comprehensible input" in course or curriculum descriptions. On the other hand, if you see an emphasis on "parts-to-whole," "grammar forms," or "translation," move on.

Luckily, there are high-quality online options that meet these criteria, such as Homeschool Spanish Academy. There are also robust networks of Saturday schools that cater to heritage speakers or to faith communities. These can be surprisingly affordable, as they are often subsidized by foreign governments or nonprofit cultural organizations. For example, a semester of weekly classes at the Chinese schools in Morgantown, WV, and Orlando, FL, runs about $250. You may also be able to find knowledgeable tutors through local colleges and universities; just be sure that the person you're considering has experience working with your child's age group.

CHAPTER 15

NOTES ON THE ARTS

When it comes to the visual, performing, and literary arts, we again want to distinguish between skills and content. Skills give students the ability to *do* an activity. Content means knowing *about* the subject on an academic level. In the visual arts, for example, it's the difference between being able to paint a flower and knowing who Georgia O'Keeffe was. Students should have access to both skills and content in the arts.

Young children are still developing fine motor skills, and the arts are perfect ways to help them do this. Pinching clay, sweeping paintbrushes, threading needles, and plunking piano keys are all ways to hone fine motor skills. Fine motor skills are critical for handwriting, being able to zip up coats, and chopping vegetables for dinner.

On the art appreciation side, reading, field trips to museums, and attending performances broaden kids' background knowledge about the fine arts, stockpiling knowledge for later use. Coffee table books of art to peruse in quiet moments; a membership to an art museum for long, gray winter afternoons; and yes, that annual trip to see "The Nutcracker," all help create an important store of background knowledge.

Your middle-grade child might want to take some kind of lessons or classes in the visual or performing arts. A high-quality fine art program will teach them elementary drawing and painting skills, allowing them to produce a reasonably life-like product. Many kids study a musical instrument or sing in a community chorus or church choir. Community theatre and local folk dance groups are other options for the performing arts, often at lower cost than private lessons. Don't overlook other options, like street dance or theatre, mural painting, puppetry, fiber arts clubs, NaNoWriMo, or open mic events.

Remember, the purpose of all this is not to produce a professional painter, musician, dancer, actor, or author—unless that's your child's goal. The idea is to equip kids with enough skills to enjoy the arts and to increase their cultural literacy and appreciation.

CHAPTER 16

NOTES ON ATHLETICS AND HEALTH

Just as making art can help young students develop their fine motor skills, athletics can help with gross motor skills. Hopping, skipping, and jumping through dance, karate, and swimming lessons—all of these build strength and coordination.

If your child is inclined toward team sports, then have them participate. Rec leagues can be an inexpensive option. Otherwise, seek out more individual opportunities to move their bodies. Personal fitness and outdoor recreational activities  provide huge boosts for both physical and mental health. Physical exercise has even been shown to improve learning.[1] Courtney recommends swimming lessons if you can at all swing the cost because it's a matter of personal safety. For children, drowning is the second leading cause of unintentional injury death.

Health is another subject you'll want to cover, either in the context of science or as a separate class under the umbrella of athletics/physical education. As a basic preparation for adulthood, your child should know how their body works and how to take care of it. This includes how babies are made (and how not to make them), how to safely prepare healthy food, how to decide what to eat and when, how to care for their mental health, how to give and ask for consent, and how to exercise for fun and self-care. An underrated part of health is safety, whether that's learning about fire extinguishers and carbon monoxide detectors or the best way to clean toilets (never mix ammonia and bleach products!).

---

1   Ratey, J J (2008) *Spark: The Revolutionary New Science of Exercise and the Brain.* Little, Brown Group.

CHAPTER 17

TESTING

We believe homeschoolers should test their children on a regular basis. Yes, we really do think that, and it's a less controversial position than some homeschoolers might assume. In fact, we bet that, if you're an academic homeschooler, you already test your kids. Does your child have weekly spelling quizzes? Do they do a review at the end of their math chapter? Those are tests.

As we saw in chapter 7, one of the best ways to help students move information into long-term memory—that is, to learn—is retrieval practice. That's what tests are: practice in recalling information.

Use Professional Assessments

We also think you should choose a curriculum with assessments written by a professional. Professional test designers are called psychometricians, and they use high-level statistical analysis to create *standardized assessments* that reliably assess a wide variety of children for given rationales. Bad assessments exist—Courtney has written some. We have also purchased relatively expensive curricula with tests on material that wasn't explicitly reviewed. Bad tests can have confusing questions, can be formatted badly, or can test trivia. Assessment is a science, and having an expert write questions is better for everyone.

Courtney tests her children every January and May. While her eldest is a quick learner and could pass the end-of-chapter tests in Singapore Math, annual tests revealed that she was not retaining the material. Her scores did not change from the January of 2nd grade to the January of 3rd grade. Courtney was worried, so she took her child in for a full neuro-educational psychological workup that spring, which revealed that her daughter had dyscalculia. Once Courtney had that piece of information, she could choose a curriculum suited for children with learning disabilities in math. Courtney would not have known to go down that path if she hadn't done the regular annual testing.

Types of Tests

For our purposes, knowing the difference between a norm-referenced test and a criterion-referenced test is important.

Norm-referenced means that the score is a percentage ranking compared to an average population. For example, Johnny is at the 45th percentile. This means if you took 100 students and ranked their scores from top to bottom, Johnny would be 45th from the bottom. Most of the legal annual testing requirements are for norm-referenced tests because state education administrators want to know how big batches of children line up with the national averages. Are Mississippi's students ahead or behind the national average in reading?

These are not bad tests, but your score report usually doesn't offer the detailed information you might want as your child's teacher. For example, we might want to know whether Tommy is just being difficult, or can he really not divide two-digit decimals?

For that kind of detailed information, we look to *criterion-referenced* tests. These tests have detailed lists of knowledge and procedures that students should know at each grade level. When your child takes these tests, they are systematically tested on each piece of information. Clearly, this is more useful to the individual homeschooling parent because we end up with dozens of pages of skills that have been checked, and so we know exactly whether Tommy can divide two-digit decimals on demand. These are the kind of tests that Courtney used to determine that her elder daughter wasn't progressing in math.

Also useful, criterion-referenced tests can report in grade level equivalent scores. For example, "Jane's phonics skills are low 4th grade level." This is a different result from a typical norm-referenced test that says "8th grade." Usually, on a norm-referenced test, that result doesn't mean that your child is working at the 8th grade level—it means that your child performed as well as an 8th grader would have on those questions.

Because there are no nationally agreed-upon progressions of knowledge outside of decoding and math (and possibly other languages), we have yet to find a grade-by-grade criterion-referenced test for science or social studies. This would require a systematic, detailed, outline of knowledge and procedures of science and social studies to be learned at each grade level, instead of a general assessment of what most students across the USA know at each grade level. (As of this writing, the state of Louisiana is tackling this issue.)

One other key piece of knowledge when selecting tests is about individualized, adaptive tests. On adaptive tests, questions change depending on whether the child got it right or wrong, becoming more or less difficult. This method has the advantage of fine-tuning the test so you know what grade level your child is actually capable of. However, there are a couple caveats.

The first caveat is that if your child answers well initially, the tests may skip ahead to higher-level knowledge and assume that your child knows something that they don't (like the multiplication table). This gives you a false positive, and frequently, a very unhappy child. Another caveat is that if the test doesn't skip ahead, your child may be in for a very long test indeed, often covering several days. Few young children have the stamina for days of testing. They often figure out they can end the test by getting it wrong, which is not a true assessment of their skills.

Criterion-referenced tests and norm-referenced tests are not the only tests, and these are not the only issues (headroom in achievement testing for gifted children is often problematic, for example). These are not even the best tests. An educational psychologist can administer much more detailed, much more thorough assessments, including screening for learning disabilities. But, norm-referenced and criterion-referenced adaptive tests can be a useful part of your homeschool planning.

Formative assessment forms your instruction. These are your checks for understanding during a lesson, your child's independent practice, and the pre-requisite knowledge checks at the beginning of the lesson. If there are any problems with these formative assessments, you'll naturally adjust your instruction to help your child learn better, right then.

Summative assessment sums up your instruction. These are the end-of-year exams, the annual standardized tests, and so on. These help you figure out how much your child knows in each subject area. While you should probably use these to guide future studies, these assessments don't immediately affect that day's teaching.

Background Knowledge Matters

We've already discussed the importance of background knowledge in the chapter on reading. In fact, many assessments are subtle tests of background knowledge. Particularly in norm-referenced tests, students are asked to read the question and select a multiple-choice answer. The mental step in between these two tasks—understanding the question—requires background knowledge.

Famously, Recht and Leslie did a reading comprehension study back in the late '80s that demonstrates this idea. Students who were good readers with lots of knowledge about baseball performed best of all, but surprisingly, students who struggled to read and had lots of knowledge about baseball came in a close second place, well above good readers with little knowledge about baseball. As Daniel Willingham notes in the Spring 2006 edition of *American Educator*, the close correspondence between background knowledge and reading comprehension test performance has been replicated many times.

	Good readers	Struggling readers
Lots of knowledge about baseball	1st place	2nd place
Little knowledge about baseball	3rd place	4th place

Beware of Writing Assessment Pitfalls

Assessing writing is particularly tricky. Dr. E. D. Hirsch, Jr.'s *The Schools We Need: And Why We Don't Have Them* describes a study from 1961, in which Paul Diederich and colleagues had hundreds of student papers assessed by dozens of graders and, "more than one third of the papers received every possible grade. That is, 101 of the 300 papers received all nine grades: A, A-, B+, B, B-, C+, C, C-, and D" (183). As homeschoolers, we don't have the advantage of 30 essays to stack up against each other, or decades of typical responses for this assignment. For these reasons, we are strong proponents of having an experienced outsider assess with a detailed rubric that looks for particular characteristics in the writing, rather than a general quality judgment.

Where to Find a Test

There is a small but reliable market for homeschoolers who wish to test their children. Online, you can find criterion-referenced tests for math and reading (Let's Go Learn's ADAM and DORA) and normed tests (Seton Testing offers several). Another online option is the MAP, which is a slightly different kind of test, widely used by school districts (Homeschool Boss offers this). You can also buy testing by mail for the normed Iowa, CAT, and TerraNova from Seton and other providers. In addition, large local homeschool organizations often offer local annual testing that complies with your state's testing requirements (if any). Generally, at the time of this writing, an annual test will set you back about $50, which is a small price to pay for peace of mind for outside proof of your child's educational progress.

Testing Procedures

Make sure your child has had plenty of sleep the night before, has food in their belly before they start, and has scratch paper and a pencil as necessary. If it's a bubble sheet, make sure your child knows how to fill in the proper bubble. Go through the introductory testing protocol with them. Your test provider will script that for you. Then step away.

Do not help your child with the exam. Do not redirect them. Do not prompt them to answer a particular question or ask them if they're sure. Do not read the test to them unless explicitly told to in the testing protocol and then only read the section that the testing protocol tells you to. Do not leave them alone to look up the answers on the Internet. Do not allow them to use a calculator unless the testing protocol tells you to. Do not add extra time to the test.

Doing any of those things invalidates the test results, giving you an inaccurate picture of what your child can actually do. Remember, at the end of the homeschooling journey, your child will have to be a self-sufficient adult, and that begins with you having a realistic picture about their capabilities.

Using the Test Results

Once you have the test results, carefully review what they show you. Generally speaking, if your child is "average" or above on a normed test (the 40th percentile or above), you can pat yourself on the back and carry on. While tests are a valuable part of assessing a child for a learning disability, these kinds of tests cannot tell you if your child has a learning disability. Only a thorough evaluation from a neuro-educational psychologist or similar professional can officially diagnose your child with a learning disability.

Given that caveat, if your child does poorly in a content area like science or social studies, you might want to re-examine your teaching methods and priorities. For example, Courtney's eldest came out of her seventh grade testing surprised by how much civics she didn't know, so they used iCivics the next year to strengthen her civics education. The next year, her civics score was much improved.

On the other hand, you may decide that you're comfortable ignoring some of the tested items. Courtney didn't feel that her then-6-year-old needed to learn about supply and demand curves before they learned how money works, so she ignored those missed questions on the test. Make sure that you're comfortable with those kinds of results, because they'll have later consequences. Everyone, from hair stylists to doctors, has to pass standardized tests at some point in life, so ensuring your child can do that is important.

Math

If your child does poorly in mathematics on a normed test, you should track down a criterion-referenced exam (we recommend Let's Go Learn's diagnostic math assessments) and nail down the gaps in their learning. Then you can adjust your child's studies to focus on things they're not good at or things they don't know. Several high-quality homeschool math curriculum providers offer targeted materials, such as RightStart Math's fractions kits and Math Mammoth's topical workbooks. Do not just let them sit there at a lower skill level until they graduate from high school. The goal is to catch your child up with the average score for their age. If math is a persistent issue (targeted, daily remediation without success), then you should probably find a neuro-educational psychologist or similar professional to assess your child for a learning disability. There are many excellent homeschool math programs. Whichever you choose, you should try to stick with it to avoid gaps.

Reading

If your child does poorly in reading comprehension or English language arts on a normed test, that's a more difficult, yet critical area to address. First, you should address their phonics knowledge. Decoding is the necessary but insufficient place to start. We recommend Let's Go Learn's diagnostic reading assessments as a first step to tackle their phonics knowledge.

If they don't do well on a decoding screener, then you're going to want to ensure they have no underlying issues, such as visual impairment or hearing loss. Your child should see an optometrist yearly anyway, but tell your optometrist that your child is having reading issues, and they can do a basic screening for visual issues at near and far. Your pediatrician should be able to do a basic screen and/or refer you to an audiologist, who should do an evaluation that lasts a couple of hours, including time in a soundproof booth. Your local school district may provide audiologist assessments as part of their legally-obligated "child-find" mandate to screen children for disabilities.

Once you've eliminated access to the curriculum as an issue, then you may need to adjust your curriculum. You may wish to make an appointment with a reading specialist if you can find one in your area. You should also look into curricula that specialize in clear teaching of reading fundamentals, typically called direct instruction phonics programs. While we wouldn't go all in on it, your child may also benefit from a little bit of practice with sight recognition.

If you have given your child a placement test for a direct instruction phonics curriculum, placed them at the correct level, and are giving them direct, explicit instruction, they should make progress. If it's been more than six months and your child hasn't made significant progress, then they may have dyslexia or other learning issues, and you need to make an appointment with a medical professional, such as a neuro-educational psychologist, for a full evaluation. Often, your pediatrician can refer you, so that health insurance will cover it. Your local school district may also provide testing services as part of their legally-obligated "child-find" mandate to screen children for disabilities. Be aware that the testing through your public school system is aimed at whether your child would have a difficulty in the classroom that would lead your child to fail to progress, not whether the difficulties exist.

While you're waiting for this, you may need to go hardcore with a program like SPIRES (3rd edition). You may also want to look into Rooted in Language or Barton, because these programs will give you access to specialists in teaching children with reading difficulties. These are significantly more expensive, both in your time and in dollars.

If your child can decode fluently and has a good foundation of background knowledge, but has difficulty with reading comprehension, they may have another, more subtle, learning disability. You need to make an appointment with a neuro-educational psychologist or similar type of medical professional for a full evaluation, and make sure you understand the recommendations they provide at the end of the evaluation. Again, your pediatrician may refer you for health insurance purposes. Your local school district is another option. While slightly rarer than hen's teeth, consultants for these kinds of learning disabilities do exist, and you may wish to work with one for your homeschool journey.

STEPS TO ENSURING YOUR CHILD CAN READ

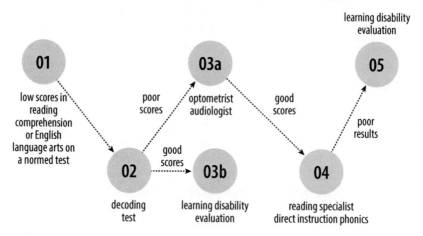

PART III

In this last section, we address common issues in homeschooling, based on our own personal and professional experiences as homeschoolers and service providers within the homeschool community. We know that homeschooling can be difficult, and in this section we shine a spotlight on some of the thornier problems. First, we address the issue of actually getting it done. Next, we lean on our own experience to discuss learning disabilities, neurodiversity, and mental health in the homeschool. Then we talk about the power of routines when schooling through a crisis, and finally, we tackle the question of when and how to navigate the transition to school.

CHAPTER 18

WHEN SCHOOL ISN'T GETTING DONE

Brittney is at her wits' end. Every time she calls him to the table to do school, her 9-year-old son, Jayden, begins whining and complaining. At first, she insisted he complete his lessons before playing, but more and more frequently, she lets him continue with his *Minecraft* game or YouTube video to avoid the unpleasantness of dealing with his angry outbursts. Besides, his 5-year-old sister is struggling with phonics, and the toddler is doing—uh-oh. Why is it suddenly so quiet? And where have the craft scissors gone?

If you've homeschooled for a while, this scenario might look familiar. Maybe a friend has shared their struggles, or you've seen something similar play out in your own home. A child resists schooling, and rather than engage in a pitched battle every day, the parent lowers their expectations little by little. Soon enough, no school has happened for a couple of months, and the child is losing ground academically. We call this phenomenon "the slide," and it's far more common than most homeschoolers want to admit.

Unfortunately, Courtney sees this all too often in her annual homeschool assessments. Parents are often quite frank about the lack of academic work their child has been doing. For example, last night Courtney reviewed a portfolio that had perhaps 30 days' worth of academic activities listed for the entire year. There were no informal academic activities, like field trips, either. The parent simply hadn't instructed the child because they were busy with other things. More often than she'd like, Courtney deals with parents who claim they are unschooling while the child spends the majority of their days watching entertainment shows on the Internet or playing video games.

Even when school does get done, it's easy to "major in the minors," and spend more time on sidelights like reading poetry, doing picture study, and going on nature walks than on the core subjects of math and writing. Parents may default to read-alouds and casual conversations rather than demand more rigorous academic output from their kids in the form of essays or lab reports. We've all seen this many times with curricula advertised as "relaxed" or "gentle."

Sometimes a parent's academic expectations genuinely are unrealistic, and the child is rebelling because the work really is over their head. No one likes to feel incompetent, and a mismatch between the child's abilities and the curriculum can lead to frustration. But far more often, the "slide" indicates an underlying issue in the parent-child relationship. By adding the role of teacher to the role of parent, the adult is taking on new responsibilities and a new area in which they exercise authority in the child's life. Since learning is often hard work, children naturally try to avoid it; who wouldn't rather play video games than memorize the capital of Bhutan? At that point, the parent needs to exert their authority in the perhaps unfamiliar and uncomfortable role of teacher, presenting a challenging adjustment for both parent and child.

Engaging Your Child's Cooperation

Child welfare has been one of Courtney's areas of concern for many years. Before she homeschooled, she was a Court Appointed Special Advocate (CASA) for abused and neglected children in the foster care system. As a certified, licensed public school teacher, an in-home vision specialist with WV Birth to Three, and then later as a 4-H Club leader and Girl Scout troop leader, Courtney was trained to identify and report child abuse and neglect. Over the years, Courtney has done hundreds of end-of-year homeschool reviews and assessments for local area homeschoolers, gaining an inside look at how others conduct their homeschools. During their time as a classroom teacher in California and New Hampshire private schools, Drew was a mandatory reporter. As a private tutor, both in person and online, they have been afforded an insider's view of dozens of homeschools around the world. Over her decades of homeschooling, Jenn has seen the long-term outcomes of homeschool and parenting choices, both for her own children and for her children's peers. In her role as a curriculum consultant, Jenn has counseled many frazzled parents who are struggling with their homeschools in these difficult times.

Parents ask us all the time, "How do I get little Timmy to sit and listen to me?" The answer is that you enforce your household rules. What do you do when little Timmy doesn't put his dirty laundry in the hamper? Homeschooling is the same problem, only about math problems instead of dirty socks. In our experience, there are two extreme responses, both of them ineffective.

If your answer is that you pick up the socks yourself and feel exasperated or resentful about it, let us suggest that you're not doing your child (or their future partner) any favors in the long run. Many parents will opt to "unschool" in order to avoid arguments with their children or what they perceive as placing undue stress on their children. This leads to the 12-year-old we learned of last week, who had never added 2-digit numbers. You must be able to ask your children to do the hard work, to push them past what they think they can do, and still maintain a good relationship with your children.

On the other hand, parents may opt to go all in on "spare the rod and spoil the child," which often leads to broken relationships, particularly when adult children are finally out from under their parents' thumbs. We know the adults these children grew into, counting some of them as employees, friends, and acquaintances. As children, these people may have so much stress that their fight or flight reflex kicks in, rendering them incapable of deep engagement with the material, limiting their learning and ultimately their adult educational and career options.

If your child has ongoing meltdowns about schoolwork, don't let them tread water below grade level for years on end or treat them harshly when they're unable to perform to your expectations. Instead, get them assessed for a learning disability or other special need. Children will rarely tell you that they don't understand because their poor vision prevents them from seeing the math book or that they don't understand the social or interpersonal assumptions left unspoken in the novel they're reading. Instead, they'll push back with a poor attitude, because they don't know that their experience is outside of normal. They need help, not punishment or low expectations. See chapter 19 for more on learning differences.

We want to be clear here: We're not perfect parents. As we share in this book, we have made mistakes of our own and will undoubtedly continue to do so. We're human. Parenting is difficult under the best of circumstances, and homeschooling only adds to that difficulty. All of us have children whose educational needs are far from average. If you need a book about parenting, *Positive Discipline* by Jane Nelson is a good start. Doing the work to establish a good relationship with your children is a critical component of homeschooling. A good relationship isn't all you need, but you can't successfully homeschool without it.

Looks Are Deceiving

Some parents try to assuage their guilt over not getting lessons done by labeling what they're doing "relaxed homeschooling" or "unschooling." We think this is unfair, both to unschoolers and to the children who are not getting the education they deserve.

There is a distinction between people who actively pursue unschooling as an educational philosophy and those who use the term to gloss over the slide into educational neglect. Lest you think we exaggerate; this spring alone Courtney has talked to more than one parent who admitted that they hadn't done any education with their child in months. They knew their children were significantly behind in academics and yet had not provided instruction of any kind. While this may shock you, we assure you that it is far from rare; all three of us have seen it repeatedly in our professional dealings with homeschooling families.

There are only 938 weeks between birth and adulthood. That may seem like a lot when our babies are a tiny bundle in our arms, but we have a deadline. While an entire school year may seem like a long time, and the 13 years of formal education may seem like forever, our children have a lot to learn before they become self-sufficient adults. During annual assessments, Courtney sees homeschoolers who've let academics slide from one day to the next, until months have passed and their third grader is reading *See Spot Run* instead of gearing up for *Bridge to Terabithia*. We don't want that to happen to you or your children.

As adults who take child welfare seriously, we think we can expect more from ourselves as home educators than putting the responsibility for education on the shoulders of a minor child. However, some families might be able to get away with it. In the *The Well-Trained Mind*, Jesse Wise quotes Dorothy Sayers:

"[E]ducation…was now running on what she called the 'educational capital."

Jessie Wise goes on to say,

> We no longer teach our children the process of memorization, organization, and expression—the tools by which the mind learns. The leftover remnants of those methods have carried us through several decades of schooling without catastrophe…But sooner or later, the capital gets used up.

When Courtney first read this, she thought it was a conservative response to what the author erroneously perceived as falling educational standards. But then she read about Pierre Bourdieu's ideal of cultural capital, and he was not at all a conservative. Later, she read about Michael F. D. Young's idea of powerful knowledge, and here again was someone who was not conservative talking about how class and knowledge are related.

We have seen parents who are brilliant enough, wealthy enough, and educated enough to have the benefits of their high socio-economic status trickle down to their children. In our experience, these are almost always the parents who will claim that passive unschooling "works" by example of their adult children. From our perspective, what "works" is that their children have been privileged with the time to develop careers as adults who could not otherwise support themselves and/or the wealth to obtain higher education despite fewer qualifications.

More commonly, in our professional practice with homeschoolers, we see children like the third grader who could not recognize all the letters of the alphabet, the tween who could not add double-digit numbers, 16-year-old who couldn't write the months of the year, and the adults in their twenties who cannot pass basic college admissions tests. Most children will not be able to easily make up these kinds of educational deficits. Popularizing this kind of "unschooling" as a valid educational philosophy while omitting family wealth and socio-economic background does homeschoolers a grave disservice.

When homeschoolers don't know that that mom with that pretty Instagram feed hires a reading tutor for her children, they might not understand what's happening when she says that she doesn't force her children to read. When she says that all she does is strew good books around the house for her children, that's technically true. However, we know that only single-digit percentages of children teach themselves to read. We're not willing to bet that our children are in those single digits, and we don't think other parents should take that bet, no matter how pretty those pictures are of children relaxed on sofas with books. Instead, we teach our children to read.

Teaching, at its core, means that we need to ask our child to recall related information. "Timmy, remember when we learned about planting seeds?" Then we present the new concept step by step, using examples and non-examples. "Did you know that almonds are seeds? Can you name another seed? Potatoes aren't seeds. Can you think of something we eat that is not a seed?" After that, we'll want to carefully monitor while our child successfully completes an initial set of problems. "Here, answer these questions. No, these questions, right here. Full sentences, Timmy." Later, we'll need to check the rest of their work. "Timmy, carrots aren't seeds." During end-of-year assessments, Courtney regularly meets with parents who send children off with a book or workbook and expect their child to learn independently. She can tell because those books and workbooks are left unfinished.

Parents often think that passive unschooling is easier than an academic approach because children will learn whatever they need to learn through everyday life. We've had parents say to us, "Listen, I'm an adult and I can't do geometry, and I'm fine." We think that's an enormous risk because you don't know if your child will one day decide that they want to be an engineer. We've seen those children trying to cram four years of high school math in one year so they can go to college. Their parents' choice to unschool has essentially handicapped those children's future prospects.

Active Unschooling

We feel that most parents underestimate how difficult it is to implement the high-quality support found in families who are actively pursuing unschooling as an educational philosophy. The parents that we know that do active unschooling well spend many thousands of dollars and hours of their time to have their children come out on the other end with a decent education, often outsourcing direct instruction to specialist mentors. Frankly, we don't have the time, money, inclination, or connections to provide our children with an ever-changing array of educational resources and activities across the entire curriculum. But our hats are off to those who do.

With active unschooling, you can't sit down and get it done every day by concentrating on an hour of this, an hour of that, and then an hour of the other thing, as academic home educators do. In reality, active unschooling is much more time-consuming because educational opportunities at your child's academic skill level have to be custom-prepared and laboriously made interesting for your child. After all, active unschooling is child-led learning, and if the child finds it unpleasant, they can and do simply get up and walk away when the going gets tough. Grit only applies when someone does something they don't want to do, a bit like bravery is feeling afraid and doing it anyway.

In our view, active unschooling is a huge gamble you're taking with your child's education. What frequently happens in active unschooling is that children become specialists. These children may well decide to spend three to five years on something that they are interested in. However, we have repeatedly found that these children are oblivious about other subjects, supplied only with random, disconnected skills instead of a general competency across disciplines.

Frequently, even given well-intentioned active unschooling parents who will do everything and buy everything to support their child's subject of interest, these children will run into trouble later in life. For example, almost all college programs require general education courses that assume at least a cursory familiarity with the academic subjects taught in public high schools. If your child has never studied science because they weren't interested in it, they will struggle mightily to pass their required STEM courses in community college. Likewise, if they lack basic background knowledge about the Constitution or the civil rights movement, that US history class will be tough going. Even reading the newspaper with understanding will prove a challenge if you can't identify the capital of China or don't recognize references to "the Kremlin" or "Capitol Hill." Yes, students can theoretically google these terms—assuming they can come up with a meaningful search string—but how many kids are going to bother to read half a dozen Wikipedia articles just to make it through a paragraph in *USA Today?* Precious few, we're betting.

"When You're Going Through Hell, Just Keep Going" — Winston Churchill

Many homeschoolers begin with a "school in a box" curriculum and then, after they get comfortable, they want to branch out. After all, you can teach anything you want! The freedom is exhilarating and fun. Many homeschooling parents express their creativity by creating lessons from scratch, often daily.

Research shows that this isn't just our perception. The longer people homeschool, the less academics they tend to do, and the lower the academic achievement of their children: a "consistent pattern of gradual decline in achievement scores the longer a child remained homeschooled."[1] We often run across long-time homeschooling parents who laugh at planning, or even finishing curricula they've purchased. Moving from teaching the oldest child explicit phonics to completely "unschooling" the youngest child is a known phenomenon—we all see it regularly.

Let us help you avoid this problem. We love to be creative, too, but instead of relying on ourselves to be creative for a year at a time, across multiple subjects, with multiple children, we use scripted curricula to give ourselves more time to be creative in other, less critical areas. That way, we can make memories and Instagram projects, but we avoid slacking off in core academic areas. Ensuring our homeschool curricula are as open and go as possible helps when our family is down for weeks with COVID, our brother-in-law moves in after his divorce, and the sewer line backs up—all at the same time. Life happens, and though some days off are unavoidable, we are still responsible for our children's education. That particular show must go on, even on mornings when our eyelids feel like sandpaper, the baby has a nasty cough, and we're fielding phone calls from the hospital billing office.

We've been there, and we know we won't have the time and energy to keep inventing math lessons in the midst of a crisis. If everything we use for teaching our children is ready for us to open and go, we can still "git 'er done" that day.

---

1 Boulton, 1999, attributes this to parental education, in *Homeschooling: An Updated Comprehensive Survey of the Research*, Kunzman and Gaither, 2020.

This Too Shall Pass

Even experienced home educators feel like quitting this job sometimes. We are not trying to hide the reality that homeschool days can get hard. Here's what we do when the lessons, arguing, and mess are too much.

First, give yourself a timeout. Take fifteen minutes without children. Make yourself a cup of your favorite beverage (ours contain some caffeine), do some breathing exercises, and quiet yourself. Let the kids have a recess, preferably in another room or outside.

Second, go outside if at all possible. We all need some Vitamin D now and then. We know, it's quite unfair that exercise helps boost bad moods. Take the horde, er, children, for a walk. If the weather doesn't cooperate, have a dance party and get those endorphins up. A lighthearted break can often reset a bad day.

Third, remember that brains are tricksy. If necessary, make a sign and put it on the refrigerator to remind yourself. Your feelings are valid, but your perspective might shift in a few hours or the next day. When you're ready to rage quit, you're probably not in the best place to make decisions. Journaling often helps us pinpoint the problem. Review what you wrote the next day and see if you still think it's true. Once you can identify the problem, you can work on a solution.

What *not* to do:

- **Go on social media and complain.** Why? You're inevitably going to draw criticism from people who don't fully understand your situation. Or, that one person will offer unsolicited advice you don't want or need.

- **Browse different curricula.** Why? In our culture, we're conditioned to see problems as situations you can buy your way out of. No amount of money will change the fact that your 8-year-old is pushing back on learning their times tables because it's hard.

- **Complain, face to face, to people who aren't supportive.** Why? They'll perceive you as someone who is incompetent and tear you down. What you need is someone who will build you up.

- **Make any immediate change.** Why? One day, or even a handful of days, is a statistical anomaly. Maybe your 10-year-old didn't sleep well last night, or your 14-year-old had a falling-out with their best friend, or your 5-year-old is coming down with a cold. Wait until an identifiable pattern emerges, then figure out how to fix the problem.

To be honest, a great many problems come from our own behavior. Most of the time, when we feel frustrated, the issue is that we haven't been consistent. Consistency and repetition are the keys to a successful home learning environment. An effective homeschooling parent uses both, in academics and in household routines.

Preparing for Independent Work

Almost all young children, by which we mean children aged ten and under, are simply not ready for most independent work. You will need to teach, closely monitor, and follow up for nearly every lesson. This is why we are not fans of online work for young children. As can be seen from assessments before, during, and after schools shut down during the pandemic, young children don't learn well online.

Most students around junior high age will continue to need supervision and direction to get their work done. Unless you have deliberately and carefully taught study skills and your child is on the upper end of the developmental spectrum, plenty of 7th and 8th graders will devolve into absolute chaos if you leave them on their own. Puberty-induced brain fog is a thing!

We've seen homeschooling parents who are still rounding up pencils and putting their children's work into their binder for them in high school. Teach middle school students study skills and teach them hard. Rather than picking up the slack by doing *for* your child, help tweens and young teens move toward ownership of their studies by providing checklists. When they get off track, gently and consistently redirect them to their to-do list. Supports like these are helpful for everyone from surgeons to fast food janitors, as Atul Gawande showed in *The Checklist Manifesto*.

Remember, by the end of high school, the average student will be a legal adult. By then, they need to have the academic skills to allow them to succeed on the job or in college. In addition, they need to be organized and self-motivated enough to function without you. Build those skills now.

Work toward autonomy, but don't leave tweens and teens completely to their own devices. This is the age where they'll fail and try to hide their failure. They'll procrastinate and then try to speed through a week's worth of work on Friday afternoon. Try to strike a balance between independence and support. Sit with them for the hard subjects, and check their work daily.

If you have children with executive function issues (common with ADHD or autism), you may need to sit with them for nearly everything. Being a warm body in the next chair is called *body-doubling* and it helps many people with ADHD to maintain focus for longer than they would on their own. Children with sensory issues may need a quiet household to focus: no dishwasher or washing machine running, no dog nails clicking on the floor or hamster wheels squeaking, and no siblings practicing instruments or playing loud games of tag. If you're lucky, you have a child who can sit with you once a week and fill out their own planner as you assign their work for the week. That way, you are both on the same page. But be honest with yourself about whether or not your child is ready for that level of independence, and if not, give them the support they need now while building the skills they need for greater autonomy.

CHAPTER 19

LEARNING DISABILITIES, NEURODIVERSITY, AND MENTAL HEALTH

Of all the chapters in this book, this one probably hits closest to home for all of us. Each of us has at least one child with a learning disability, a neurological difference, or a mental health diagnosis—sometimes all three.

We know we're not alone. Not only are these issues common in the general population, but we suspect that they are overrepresented among homeschoolers. Why? Public schools do not have a great track record of teaching children who fall outside the middle of the bell curve, let alone those who seem to turn the bell upside down! We've observed that many people turn to homeschooling when IEPs and 504 plans don't help, or aren't implemented properly.

However, we've also seen many homeschoolers who resist having their children professionally evaluated despite multiple signs of disability and ongoing academic and personal struggles. Perhaps because they don't have access to a large pool of average children to compare their own to, they aren't entirely aware of their child's differences. They may erroneously believe that, if their child is diagnosed, they won't be able to homeschool anymore. Some families lack the resources to pay for formal evaluations, as insurance plans may not cover them unless the family can prove that the child's education is negatively affected by their condition—something that can be difficult to do without the observations of people outside the family, like school teachers or coaches.

The odds are good, but the goods are odd.

Courtney took her youngest child on a homeschool field trip last week. After going through the diagnosis process for special education needs with both of her own children plus working in special education for several years, she has a decent eye for the neurodivergent among us. Courtney traded sympathies with a mother who'd forgotten her child's noise-canceling headphones and watched another parent balance a fearful child on one hip while holding the hand of another. In a public school classroom, those would be the problem children, but in a homeschool group, they blended in.

In our experience, homeschoolers are often significantly more tolerant of differences than the average population. That's because homeschoolers are people who march to their own beat. Frankly, sending your child to school is the easy option. Everybody does it, nobody judges you for it, and 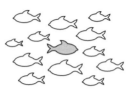 your child is guaranteed some minimal amount of care for six or seven hours a day. Swimming upstream against a strong current of school photos and award ceremonies is not a fun time.

Most homeschoolers who stick with it for the long-term do so because they believe it's the best available option for their child. Why would anyone do it if they thought their child would be worse off in the end? Many children who are homeschooled are neurodivergent or different in some other way from the average schoolchild and their caregivers feel (often with solid experience to back them up) that their child would not be successful in a classroom setting. Educational choices can vary even within families—about half of homeschoolers send one or more children to a brick-and-mortar school.

Will homeschooling by itself make your child "weird"? No. Will children who are different from the norm in some way thrive in homeschooling? Quite possibly. Correlation does not indicate causation.

Socialization

Experienced homeschoolers know "What about socialization?" is the wrong question. Sending your child to school doesn't guarantee "socialization," especially these days with silent lunches and hallways, SLANT discipline,[1] and the ills of wider society that  spill into the classroom. The right question is, "What kind of socialization does your child need to be happy?" and the answer is, "It depends on your child."

Homeschooled children run the gamut from the chatterbox happily spending afternoons making new friends at the playground to the self-contained, introspective type who maintains long-term friendships through Skype and Discord. Neither of these children is "bad" at friendship. They're simply different individuals with different needs. The joy and beauty of homeschooling is the ability to be flexible in meeting your child's needs.

---

1 "Sit up, Lean forward, Answer questions, Nod your head, and Track the speaker."

Depending on your child's needs, you may wish to sign them up for sports teams and dance classes that allow them to participate on an equal footing with other, non-homeschooled children. Theater is often a refuge for children who are different in some way and usually homeschooler friendly. Groups such as Girl Scouts, 4-H, and chess club are another opportunity for socializing with peers outside of schools. Libraries are often wonderful sources of group activities, with book clubs, story times, D&D clubs for children, crafting class, and maker spaces. Other classes might be helpful as well: small-group art lessons, language classes, and athletics are all great ways for your child to spend time with other children their age.

Slightly older children can often socialize through volunteer activities. Many organized clubs have a volunteer component. Children can also volunteer in their areas of interest. For example, if your child loves animals, they might want to volunteer at an animal shelter. If they love to read, the library might have an opportunity for them to volunteer, either as a regular participant for story hours or a teen volunteer in another capacity. Giving back to the community can be important for your child.

In the end, the best activities for your children depend on your individual child.

Accentuate the Positive; Eliminate the Negative

If you're coming out of a public school with an Individual Education Plan (IEP), then you might be focused on your child's weaknesses. This is an unfortunate side effect of a system that's built around making sure that children read and do math on their grade level. When your child doesn't, then most of the time and attention ends up being on their weaknesses. This often makes a child dislike school, or feel that they're "bad" at school. As a secondhand effect, you may feel like a bad parent.

We want to offer an observation: Most adults find careers that work with their strengths. For obvious reasons, few people stay in a job they're bad at. True, you can be merely adequate and keep your job in many organizations, but life is more satisfying when you enjoy what you do—or, at least, are not terrible at it. All of this is to say, "Yes, you should eliminate your child's academic inadequacies as much as possible, but it's at least as important to hone their strengths." Those strengths are what will carry them through adulthood.

For example, as a teenager Courtney's husband was hyperfixated on being a professional writer and on videogames—and he worked hard at both of them, honing his skills. Deeply impractical, yes? Well, not as much as you'd think. Starting at age sixteen with a cold call to an editor, he was able to make a living for over a decade as an independent video game journalist. Then he moved into other nonfiction writing as a technical writer for another decade or so, and finally into data analysis. His core interest in writing and analyzing technology has paid off throughout his entire professional career.

Drew also wanted to be a writer and a teacher. They went the more traditional academic route to achieve the latter goal, only to discover that the job market for their area of specialization was virtually non-existent. Drew took a year to regroup, enrolling in a certificate course in publishing with a concentration in editing. Certificate in hand, they landed an editing job at a small publishing company in San Francisco while teaching at the local German-language school on the weekends. Over the years, Drew has used their writing, editing, and teaching skills to publish books and curricula, help found a private classical academy, and work as a private academic tutor, while also writing and publishing fiction and poetry.

As a homeschooler, chip away at your child's academic weaknesses, bit by bit, over the course of your school year. You don't need to make your third grader feel like a bad person because they don't know the definition of a noun. Similarly, you don't need to make your fourth grader with dyscalculia do long division when they haven't memorized their multiplication tables. Just fix it. Remediate those weaknesses with topical studies that meet your child's needs. As the educator-in-charge, it's more important that your child make *good progress* throughout the whole year than the progress be on grade level.

Support your child's strengths. They're a good reader? Great! Level up their assigned reading to a challenge level. They're excellent at math? Fantastic! Grab a copy of Beast Academy or compact Khan Academy for them. They love tinkering with engines? Excellent! Have them practice their expository writing on small engine repair. Whatever their interest is, support them with documentaries, trade books, and hands-on experiences as much as possible. Find them a mentor in their area of interest.

For example, Courtney's eldest wanted to be a paleontologist, so Courtney bought a membership to the Carnegie Natural History Museum and they spent many happy hours there. One of the paleontologists in residence even gave them a "backstage tour" of the museum! The career goals of Courtney's eldest have changed slightly over the years, but that early support has encouraged her to try harder at math because she knows she'll need it for a degree in biology.

Accentuating the positive helps you be a better homeschooling parent by supporting the child you have, not the child you want. While we're sure it's nice to have an extroverted, attractive genius with Olympic-caliber athletic skill as a child, the rest of us need to educate the children we have. Then those children will need to go out into the world and support themselves, whether as a trusted mechanic with a customer service list a mile long, a paleoartist who creates museum displays, or a freelance graphic designer running their own business.

Differently Wired

Most people are *neurotypical*, which simply means that their brains work like typical people's brains work. Neurotypical people don't need to think about how their brains work because they grow and develop when and how pediatricians and other specialists think they should. This makes their lives a little easier.

If your child is *neurodivergent*, their brain might function a bit differently from a typical child their age. This is not, in itself, a problem, especially when you homeschool. If your child has a poor auditory working memory and needs to have everything written down, you can do that. Conversely, if they have a reading comprehension disorder and don't retain written information very well, then you can emphasize conversations and video tutorials as their primary content learning mode.

There are some common ways in which brains diverge from the neurotypical population. For example, autism often includes differences in communication, executive function, and special interests. Autistic people are often detail-oriented, intensely focused, and creative thinkers. Another common neurodivergence is Attention Deficit Hyperactivity Disorder (ADHD), an attention regulation disorder that often results in difficulties with executive functions like self-awareness, self-restraint, working memory, emotional regulation, self-motivation, and planning. On the other hand, ADHDers can be charismatic, high-energy, and original thinkers. Still other neurodivergent people include, but are not limited to, those with dyslexia, dyspraxia, dyscalculia, and Tourette's Syndrome.

We want to emphasize that neurodivergence is not a "learning style." Learning styles are bunk. You do not need to tailor your teaching to your child's supposed "learning style." You do not need to buy curriculum advertised as appropriate for "visual" or "kinesthetic" learners—and we'd actually suggest that you run fast and far if you see that kind of marketing because it indicates that the curriculum provider doesn't know much about education. Find this suspicious? Ask a cognitive scientist. We suggest Daniel Willingham's excellent videos and articles on the subject.

Keeping in mind that we are not medical professionals, we would like to suggest that there are some clues that your child might not be typically developing. For example, we've had children kicked out of Montessori preschools for failure to understand the unspoken adult-enforced rules of "child-led learning." We've had children unable to tolerate violin lessons or dance classes due to sensory issues: violin strings are sharp, and tights are, well, tight. If your child displays clinginess and whines about attending group activities, then you might be dealing with a child who is different. (Drew notes that a child's diagnosis may lead parents to uncover their own neurodivergence.)

Neuropsychological Testing

If you suspect that your child might be neurodivergent, have a learning disability, or is developing atypically, we strongly encourage you to get your child tested by a neuro-educational psychologist or other appropriate medical professional. Your child's pediatrician can usually make a referral. If they're unwilling or unable to make the referral, look for a neuropsychologist, a doctoral level clinical psychologist who specializes in these kinds of evaluations. A qualified  neuropsychologist will offer an intensive evaluation, typically 8-12 hours of your time. Make sure that the professional you choose understands how to assess twice-exceptional children (children who are both learning disabled and gifted), because their test results vary in a way that some professionals are unfamiliar with.

Prepare your anxious child by sharing the schedule and types of tests with them in advance. Be explicit about what the testing is for and how the results will help your child. You may even wish to practice visualization exercises with your child so that unknowns don't trip their anxiety.

Frequently, the process is broken up over three days.

- **Day 1**: On the introduction day, an experienced neuropsychologist will often ask for your child's medical history, social history, and family history. Normally, this day will include symptom checklists completed by adults who know your child well, your impression of your child's strengths and weaknesses, and a discussion about whatever neurodivergence you're asking about testing for. Between that visit and the next, the neuropsychologist will prepare certain tests for your child.

- **Day 2**: On the testing day, common tests include rating scales for social, emotional, and psychiatric problems, intelligence tests, specific ability tests, and computer-based tests. Brain scans are rarely involved. Before the next meeting, the neuropsychologist will write up a lengthy report based on the results of those tests.

- **Day 3**: On the third day, they'll review the test results with you, and offer an action plan to manage the results. Ask as many questions as you need to ensure that you understand the results.

While these professionals are busy people, you need to fully understand the results because the evaluator can tell you whether your child has a learning disability, a low or high IQ, a difference like ADHD or autism, and many other critical pieces of information. Do not leave the office without making sure you understand what the evaluator is saying to you; you can't properly advocate for your child if you don't understand the issues involved in their diagnosis.

The action plans should include accommodations to help your child perform well (academically and otherwise), a plan for follow-up therapy with a therapist or similar professional, a referral for medication (if appropriate), and a schedule of follow-up appointments with your pediatrician to see how well the plan is working. If the action plan is missing or doesn't offer suggestions for accommodations, you can and should push back and ask for those items. Those are a key portion of the report.

Accommodations are critical for you to help your child in the homeschool or in any school they might attend later. Very often, your child is capable of succeeding with appropriate support. Typically, an evaluator's diagnosis will help guide not only your homeschool, but testing accommodations, services from Medicaid and the Division of Vocational Rehabilitation, and other important items for your child's future.

Dyslexia, dysgraphia, dyspraxia, dyscalculia, and other less common issues all have best practices for supporting your child in their learning. For example, students with dysgraphia might need someone to scribe their math work, so they can concentrate on mathematics instead of writing down problems. Alternatively, a student with dyslexia should have content area information provided in audio format, so that they aren't struggling to read dense texts that they're otherwise capable of understanding. This is why you should ensure that the report includes not only a diagnosis, but specific recommendations for future support.

Less careful professional offices frequently have wrong names in copy-pasted areas, and if that happens you should ask for a new report that has been double-checked for accuracy. We have also had success in pushing back against what we saw as a potential misdiagnosis. This matters because your very expensive report is the justification for medication prescriptions, testing accommodations, IEPs, and so much more. Your child deserves to have their name accurately printed in the report, and to have an accurate diagnosis.

Frequently, psychologists and other professionals will offer an "informal" diagnosis that they can't justify with their testing and won't write down. You should pay careful attention to these off-the-cuff statements. Experienced professionals can identify areas of concern that can drastically affect how you deal with your child. Many times, we've seen these "informal" diagnoses borne out by later testing.

Because testing is such a lengthy process, without insurance coverage these evaluations can run into thousands of dollars. If you make a request in writing to the special education director for your local school district, they should offer a more limited evaluation without out-of-pocket costs. Check your state's policies for how to set this "child find" process in motion through the school district.

If you're not offered a lengthy evaluation, go elsewhere, because a rushed visit may lead to a misdiagnosis or missing a secondary, underlying issue. One example is when a busy professional may diagnose the symptoms and not the underlying problem. How? Children are regularly misdiagnosed with a mood disorder when they actually have ADHD because hormonal changes at puberty exacerbate the mood dysregulation that is part of ADHD. Sometimes, medication for ADHD can dramatically improve mood issues in affected children. It's also important to know that your child can't be too smart (or too low on the IQ scale) to be diagnosed with a difference like ADHD or autism and that your child doesn't have to fail academically (or otherwise) to be dramatically affected.

Joy in the World

You might be afraid for your child, and that's normal. If you admit that your child is neurodivergent then you might think your child is broken or doomed to a miserable, unhappy life. That's simply not true. We personally know plenty of happy, healthy neurodivergent adults who live meaningful, joyful lives—including ourselves. If you have a couple dozen pages of a professional evaluation, you can use that information to better support your child's learning and eventual adult success.

Here's a bit of news that may be a surprise: If your child is neurodivergent, the chances that you are neurodivergent are quite high. Even if you were not diagnosed in school, the diagnosing standards have changed since then. In addition, we now know that neurodivergence has been overlooked in certain populations, like women and non-white people. Coming to grips with your own neurodivergence helps you be a better homeschooling parent, because you can recognize behaviors and characteristics and deliberately teach your child coping mechanisms that you have developed.

One key skill that you can teach your child is self-advocacy. Have them practice with you first. "Mom, you forgot to put my math checklist in the folder. I don't know what to do today!" Later in life, they can take those skills and use them to politely ask a supervisor for a checklist for a complicated task. Teach your child to ask if their instructor (you or someone else) can review papers before they turn them in. This practice will serve them well all the way through graduate school and into the work environment. Another good practice is to teach your child to email their instructors in advance, giving them a heads-up about their neurodivergence.

Feel free to include chores on those assignment lists. Not only will having your children do chores save you valuable time, doing chores is associated with executive function gains, especially important for many neurodivergent children.[2] Self-care chores, like doing their own laundry, and family-care chores, like cooking and gardening, are particularly helpful because they're complex tasks with multiple steps. Remember, however, that your neurodivergent children may need significant scaffolding to plan the task, get started on the task, remember how to do the task, and then switch to a new task. Verbal review of a written or picture-based checklist can be helpful before they start. Having children learn to be an independent adult capable of taking care of their own needs is a good goal.

A big family wall calendar can help keep everyone on track, especially if your child, prone to executive function difficulties, can mark important upcoming assignments and dates. By the end of high school, they should be creating their own planner. Building habits takes longer for children with executive functioning issues. You may be sitting down with them every day for six months before they can take independent control of their planner. Help them build routines into their day, like getting home from sports practice, taking a shower, eating dinner, taking their evening medications, and then preparing

2   Tepper, D L, Howell, T J and Bennett, P C (2022) "Executive functions and household chores: Does engagement in chores predict children's cognition?", *Australian Occupational Therapy Journal*, 1-14.

work and their planner for the next day. Yes, your homeschooled child may have homework, particularly for online classes.

Another key way to help them become independent is to show them how to sort through information, both in paper form and in their email. Teach your child to sort through all the incoming paperwork, both electronic and hard copy, every day. Have your child discard or file the items that don't require anything, transfer appointments or due dates to a planner, and then prepare an action checklist for the next day.

Sleep hygiene is a vital and often overlooked part of educating children about health and self-care. Neurodivergent children are notorious for having difficulty sleeping. "I wish my brain had an off switch" is a regular comment. Believe it or not, certain non-  stimulant ADHD medications are often taken in the evening to help a restless brain sleep. Ruthlessly ensure that your child wakes up at the *same time every day*, no matter how late they stayed up the night before. Vibrating alarm clocks, auto-snooze clocks, and so on are all useful.

Neurodivergent children frequently have speech delays. As homeschoolers, we may be less aware of this issue because we live with our children and can often anticipate their needs without requiring significant verbalization. However, being unable to communicate more precisely can be immensely frustrating for children, leading to frequent meltdowns. While we recommend consulting a speech language pathologist, there might be a waiting period before you can see one. In that time, you might implement alternative forms of communication, such as sign language. Even now, Courtney's children will comfortably sign in noisy environments. Another alternative is a card system. For example, Courtney made picture cards of the foods she commonly kept in the house, and her child could choose one card from each group (fruit, vegetable, protein, carbohydrate) to choose their meals. There are also Augmentative and Alternative Communication (AAC) apps for tablets that can be helpful. Communication is about more than speaking. Empowering your children with as much communication ability as possible will improve your relationship and their ability to do academics.

An accommodation that is much easier to implement at home is flexible seating. Does your child want to jump rope while they recite their multiplication tables? Go for it! Would an indoor trampoline in your living room help keep your wiggly child focused during retrieval practice? Worthwhile investment! Does your child need a super quiet space to work, possibly with noise-canceling headphones? We've done that too. Their seat is always preferential, right at your elbow while you sit with them.

Have you ever heard the saying, "You catch more flies with honey than vinegar"? This is often doubly true for neurodivergent children. Studies show that they receive many times more pieces of negative feedback than positive feedback, and are more sensitive to the negative feedback.[3] Setting up a behavior management plan that emphasizes reward over punishment might be more effective in your homeschool. However, you must follow through in order for this system to be effective. If your children distrust your follow-through, then they will not even try. For an example of a reward emphasis, to level up one of her young children in self-control, Courtney promised that if they went the entire 11-week summer without a temper tantrum (which is distinct from a meltdown), she would buy them an axolotl. It worked! There is now an axolotl in a tank in Courtney's house, and her child gained confidence in their ability to manage their temper. Teaching your children to set reasonable goals and rewards for themselves is a life skill that could serve them well.

If you're feeling crafty, you can color code daily and weekly assignment folders. Courtney made her child a color-coded box with her Cricut to keep a small set of tools all in one place, but she could easily have used a shoebox. There have been days when we wrote grammar definitions on the living room windows and diagrammed sentences on the giant mirror in the living room. We currently have a shower curtain with the periodic table on it. Whatever you need to do to help your child learn, no matter how unorthodox, is fine.

Good Results Require Hard Work

Let's be clear that if your child has special needs, you're going to have to put in significant amounts of extra time and effort for your child to reach the same level of academic achievement as a child without special needs—to the extent that that is possible for your child. The more unique your child's learning needs, the less likely it is that open-and-go lessons will work for your child.

When your child has specific learning issues, they will almost always benefit from direct instruction. Direct instruction means that you make sure that your child has a daily review, like flashcards. You'll present new material using small steps, checking for understanding throughout the lesson. You'll provide models, whether it's dissecting flowers so they can see and touch the anthers and stamens,

3   Frye, D (2020) "Children with ADHD Avoid Failure and Punishment More Than Others, Study Says", *Additude Magazine*, www.bit.ly/3wo5JFT

or partially worked examples of quadratic equations. You'll guide their practice. "No, you missed a step. What should you have done?" If it's tricky, then you'll need to scaffold the assignment, like teaching them acronyms for the order of the planets or identifying several cities on a map then asking the child to label the others. Only after they're successful with you by their side should you send them off to work by themselves.

All of this is easier said than done, so we encourage you to buy a high-quality scripted curriculum that has these techniques built into it.

Homeschooling a Child with a Complex, Chronic Health Condition

When your child is in and out of therapy services all day, your homeschool will be different, and that's OK! You are to be congratulated for getting all those services in place for your child. Those are vital for your child's future success.

Give yourself and your child some grace. Occupational therapy, speech therapy, physical therapy, and so on can take a lot out of your child. Each of those appointments comes with one-to-one instruction that is typically quite demanding. Since you've outsourced them, you've ideally got your child well-rested, awake, dressed, and fed before you've shown up at the office. With a child with a complex, chronic health condition, that can be an accomplishment in itself.

Because your homeschool day is built around your child's therapies, you can't do all the same kinds of academics as other people. Again, that's fine. You and your child are doing important work. What you need to do is prioritize, and we're going to advise learning to read and math as the two critical, must-do subjects. You may find that you need to outsource these to specialists, as well. For example, speech language therapists can help with phonics.

Save social studies and science as audio books in the car, read-alouds before bed, or as field trips (if you can swing them.) High-quality, structured discussion can help your child retain information, particularly if you repeat some items. At Courtney's house, the same books are read aloud at bedtime every Thanksgiving, for example. The books are generally over the head of young children, but by the third or fourth year, the information starts to sink in.

We promise that as your child graduates from different therapies, they'll make academic strides. Don't feel guilty about prioritizing those therapies as the center of your days.

Keeping Up with the Joneses

When you decide to homeschool your children, your relationship with them changes. It's not better or worse, but the closeness with your children is not the same as only being their parent. Jenn's family had a joke that their mother would not like to hear  about their dawdling. Jokes aside, remember to put on your "teacher hat" when you are preparing and instructing, not your "parent hat." Why? If you spend time browsing through homeschooling groups, then you'll inevitably come across descriptions of other people's children achieving much more than your children. Remember how you felt as a new parent when you compared toddler milestones at playgroup? Mm-hmm. You feel us, right?

The National Association of Gifted Children (NAGC) defines gifted children as:

> those who demonstrate outstanding levels of aptitude (defined as an exceptional ability to reason and learn) or competence (documented performance or achievement in top 10% or rarer) in one or more domains. Domains include any structured area of activity with its own symbol system (e.g., mathematics, music, language) and/or set of sensorimotor skills (e.g., painting, dance, sports).

This is kind of technical, but the upshot in terms of homeschooling is that gifted children commonly learn more easily, more quickly, and with less practice.

Most children are not gifted. Not all of our children are gifted—although some of them are. Our children do have their special interests and talents, even if they don't fit the technical definition for giftedness. That's okay! Average is wonderful! In fact, being average makes homeschooling much easier than when children are at either end of the academic spectrum.

Think that's a strange thing to say? In our experience, gifted children commonly accelerate through curriculum. A parent homeschooling a gifted child may end up buying a year's worth of curriculum every six months, or even every three. They may need to buy two advanced curricula at once just to keep their child sufficiently challenged. On the other hand, a parent homeschooling a child with a learning issue may search fruitlessly for a curriculum that breaks things down enough and also contains enough practice for their child. If the parent of a child with a learning issue finds this magical curriculum, it's often horrendously expensive, deeply complicated, and may require a specialist trained to teach it. Either way, children outside of the "typical" range require more from their homeschooling parents.

Another, more subtle point is often overlooked: Many parents of children with learning issues have those same issues themselves. If your child is gifted, you are often gifted, too, and so unfamiliar with how the "typical" child behaves and learns. If your child has a learning difference, the odds are good that you also have a learning difference. As a result, you may not perceive that your giftedness or other learning difference affects both your perception of how children learn and what the "typical" homeschool day looks like. This can lead to you not getting your child assessed for a learning difference, even when you both could use some assistance.

We frequently see parents in homeschooling groups recommending curricula that contain almost no retrieval practice, or any but the most superficial review, and swearing that they've successfully used these materials in their own homes. They probably have. But, what they don't say is that they and their children are academically gifted, or that their standards are lower than yours, or both. Asking a bunch of strangers on the Internet about what materials you should use with your particular child is a crapshoot. Sure, you can do it to get leads, but don't go hitting that purchase button merely on the recommendation of a handful of people in the group. We get it—you're tired and you just want to get it done, but resist the urge.

Choosing Curricula for Gifted Students

According to the National Association for Gifted Children, there are several main approaches to teaching gifted children.[4] The first approach is *acceleration*, or when children simply move through the curriculum faster than usual. This may mean starting formal academics earlier than usual, skipping grade levels in curricula, or even attending college early (either through *dual enrollment*— taking a college class in high school—or *early graduation*: graduating from high school at 16, for example).

Another form of acceleration is moving through a content area faster than usual, known as *curriculum compacting*. That might be implemented by quizzing a child using the weekly or chapter quizzes until they can't do the material, and then starting there. Often, a gifted child will quickly learn the material and be ready for the next quiz faster than a typical child. Parents can spend considerable time and money ensuring their child has a suitable curriculum.

The third option is really only applicable if you live in a densely populated area. This option is *grouping*, or having your child learn something with other gifted

---

4   National Association for Gifted Children, *Gifted Education Strategies*, www.bit.ly/3pAPdhX

children. For example, parents might hire a mathematics tutor for a group of middle school children who are ready to learn calculus, or have their children test into an advanced level orchestra. Summer camps for gifted children are another popular way that parents can make this happen.

Implementing Curricula

All children, whether they are gifted, typical, or with other learning differences, will succeed with an evidence-informed curriculum that includes interleaved, interval-spaced review and repetition, particularly when that curriculum is scripted by an expert in that field. Good teaching is good teaching for all children.

You may find such a curriculum to be incredibly boring and aesthetically displeasing, but just because you're bored doesn't mean that your child will be bored or fail to progress. Remember, noting that your child learned something with a bad curriculum doesn't mean that they couldn't have learned more, with less effort, with a better curriculum. Good teaching is effective and easier for you and your children. Here are three hypothetical examples:

This is Skylar's first year homeschooling. She is studying English grammar with First Language Lessons 4. *She hadn't had any grammar in her public school and usually takes two weeks to master each lesson. Her dad doesn't stress about this. Instead, he marks where they are in the teacher manual every day. To aid in retrieval practice, her dad helped her to make review cards they use for daily practice.*

Patricia has been homeschooling since kindergarten and also uses First Language Lessons 4. *Since it's her fourth year in this curriculum series, it's mostly a review for her. Despite this, her mom makes sure Patricia gets daily retrieval practice. Because Patricia knows the material well, sometimes they cover a week's worth of lessons in a day. This is fine because they need to spend extra time doing math this year.*

Jessie is the third homeschooler in her family to use First Language Lessons 4. *At this point, her parent has almost memorized it. Jessie wasn't reading fluently until recently, but because her parent was familiar with the curriculum, they adapted the lessons for purely oral work. As a result, Jessie memorized much of the grammar knowledge base without being able to read the lessons. Now that Jessie is done with phonics, she can start diagramming. This takes up most of the lesson time, since that's a new skill for Jessie.*

These families use the same curriculum, with the same scripted lesson plan, despite the children having wide differences in academic achievement. Scripted curricula do not imprison you as a teacher any more than an actor is limited by their script. Instead, a scripted curriculum gives you, the homeschooling parent, a base to adapt for your own child's needs. If you feel comfortable with the subject, go ahead and adlib from the script written in the manual. Conversely, if you aren't sure how to explain a concept, you can read it exactly as written. Either way, you are less likely to get behind or skip days when you know that your materials are open and go.

Mental Health Issues

Mental health issues are a common stumbling point among homeschoolers for the simple reason that mental health issues are pervasive in our society, knowing no class, race, or gender boundaries. It could be your mental health or your child's or both that are affecting your homeschooling. We acknowledge that this is a tricky subject to give advice on because everyone has a different situation to manage. That said, many of the tips in the section on neurodivergent learners apply equally to children with common mental health conditions such as anxiety. No one learns well if they are in a state of emotional dysregulation, so you'll want to do whatever the child needs (or you need!) to return to a calm state before asking them to learn.

All that said, Jenn can share the following tips:

Any humans are going to do well with a routine. It's going to be easier for you and your kids if you know what subjects you tackle on Tuesday and that you start back at 1 pm after lunch each day.

Build some padding into your homeschool year for those times where you are adjusting med dosages. It will happen and having a bunch of planned slush days will help you in staying positive about the situation. Also, don't change your curriculum during a time of flux. If your brain or their brain isn't operating at full speed, don't make a change to your materials or methods then.

Take advantage of your best hours. If you take an ADHD med and you know it will wear off by 3 pm, schedule school to be over by that point. It may seem obvious, but really it's sometimes hard for adults to remember to take care of our own needs.

Plan the same way for your children and their attention span. Drew once had a tutoring student whose attention for academic work was shot by 1 pm, so his mother scheduled his schoolwork in the morning, saving athletics and music for afternoons. Jenn had a situation where one kid needed to sleep late so she worked with the others in the morning and then with him in the early afternoon. Be flexible; there's no reason you can't do school later in the day or on weekends. There are no homeschool police that will fine you for doing school outside of normal school hours.

You've Got This

It's not easy to homeschool any child, but children with learning differences, neurodivergences, or mental health issues may need even more attention, care, and patience than other children. We know from personal experience how challenging it can be to keep your own anxiety about your child's well-being under control while juggling therapy appointments, med changes, and meltdowns. We hope this chapter has given you some information as well as some affirmation.

CHAPTER 20

CRISIS SCHOOLING AND FINDING YOUR "GOOD ENOUGH"

Readers who began homeschooling during COVID probably have a painfully clear sense of what "crisis schooling" means. We're using the term to refer not just to surviving a global pandemic, but to anything that throws you off your homeschooling game for more than a week. That includes everything from a new baby to juggling parental work schedules to family health or legal crises to the global chaos we've seen with the pandemic and climate disasters. We want to get you out of crisis mode and into a workable new normal that allows you to continue to give your kids the excellent education they deserve.

We openly acknowledge that that's not always possible, and that sometimes "good enough" is all you can do. Our experience has taught us that two factors—scripted open-and-go curriculum and regular household routines—are your best insurance when chaos strikes. Be compassionate with yourself and your children, but if the crisis looks like it's not going to be over soon, find a way to keep moving your children's education forward no matter what. (And if that's really not possible, see the next chapter.)

Jenn's Story

We began homeschooling in 2001 and are still homeschooling now. During these years we schooled through moves, sickness, two house fires, and the care of several elderly family members through old age, sickness, and finally hospice. Addiction and mental health issues run rampant on both sides of our families, and even our own young adult children struggle to this day.

Overall, our family has enjoyed homeschooling, but things didn't always go smoothly. Looking back, there were several time periods when I should have utilized the public school system more than we did.

Our third son, Reilly, was diagnosed with a seizure disorder and ADHD when he was seven. He needed to sleep until he woke up every day, since any kind of sleep deprivation brought on seizures.

I used as much open-and-go curriculum as possible, but I had to bend it to fit my individual students' abilities. One of my kids eventually went to public school, so I've been on that side of the fence too: IEP meetings and getting ADHD medications okayed to be brought to school because he needed such a high dosage none would last the entire school day. Managing an ADHD teen is work as a parent, and it wasn't much less than if he had stayed at our homeschool.

Your Secret Weapon: Routine

Homeschooling is working a full-time job in your home with your children. To make it more difficult, you are all there in your house, every single day. Jenn used to say that she could do only two things well every day—cook meals, keep the house mostly clean, or teach well—and she needed to do all three. In reality, something had to give every day. It took Jenn years to work out a system for homeschooling five children and keeping a clean house. The books *Atomic Habits* and *The Power of Habit* explain how to use "hooks" and automated routines to build new habits. Here are a few useful insights.

- **Routines are hard to establish.** This might be counterintuitive—if a routine saves you time, why won't it save you time now? First, you must form that routine into an automatic habit.

  Think about learning to tie your shoes. In the beginning, you were slow and clumsy and probably often whined about it. For parents, it's easier and quicker to tie the shoes yourselves. But if you give in, you'll end up with a 10-year-old who needs help putting on their shoes after a group bowling outing, and both you and the child will be ashamed of their incompetence. Instead, have your child practice shoe tying every morning as part of your morning work. After a few weeks, they will automate shoe tying—or they won't, and you should call an occupational therapist. Only after the habit is automatic will the newly acquired skill of shoe-tying save you time.

- **Routines vary in complexity, and thus in time it takes to establish them.** Putting your wallet and keys in a bowl as you walk in the door is fairly simple, so it might only take a week or two to establish the habit. Automating the routine of your math program is much more difficult and can easily take six to eight weeks of daily practice.

- **Routines are especially beneficial for people with executive function issues.** Small children are notorious for their poor decision-making skills, in part because their prefrontal cortexes are immature. Children with ADHD, autism, anxiety, and other issues also have trouble remembering to do things that aren't in their daily habits. Making important items like tooth-brushing and multiplication flashcards part of their routines will help them in the long run.

- **You are the routine enforcer.** Don't blame the children if they fail to implement the routine. Making sure the routine happens is your job. If you have trouble remembering the routine, write it down or buy an Alexa or Google Home and make it remind you. Better yet, make a visual schedule with icons for each item and tape the schedule where it will stare you in the face. The bathroom mirror at Courtney's house held an eight-step list of bathroom habits for years. We also have daily checklists for each subject, not just for the children, but for us teachers.

As a parent, there is another key aspect to establishing a new routine, and that is your children (and you!) will not enjoy establishing the new routine. Almost inevitably, your children will push back by whining and complaining, or even temper tantrums. This is perfectly normal and to be expected. You are pushing them out of their comfortable habits and nobody likes to be uncomfortable. Stay calm and confident that you do know best, that this new routine is best for your family.

Trust us when we tell you that instilling the habit of your four- or five-day academic week is key to your success. If you can start during the summer before you begin more formal academics in the autumn, work on the habit of starting the day. This will be hard for both your 5-year-old and your 15-year-old. However, knowing what comes first, second, and third on academic days makes life easier for all of you.

Routines in the Homeschool

In the morning, instilled habits help create smooth transitions. Setting the table is a natural precursor to meal times. "When the plates are on the table, we will eat shortly." Depending on your household, you may want to have hair and teeth brushed after breakfast, and then dishes loaded in the dishwasher. After that, at Jenn's house, arriving in the living room signifies the day's start. We didn't say dressed! We homeschoolers guard our self-given right to spend the entire day in pajamas!

Like many people, Jenn is a fan of beginning the day with a read-aloud. Many people read books during lunch, but she likes eating and she hasn't figured out how to read aloud and eat at the same time. Also, some of the people at her house just might be attached to their lunchtime TV show.

Courtney has a slightly different start to the day. Her children get themselves out of bed and the oldest feeds herself breakfast. The youngest sits quietly with her tablet while Courtney makes breakfast (and coffee!). After the plates are cleared, Courtney prefers to start the day in the dining room with the hardest subject, math. Everything else is easy by comparison.

Drew's daughter has never been an early riser, and Drew likes their morning quiet time, so when the two were homeschooling, they often didn't begin lessons until 10 am. In high school, they shifted to afternoons to accommodate teenage sleep patterns. Even if the timing looked different, there were still routines. Subjects got tackled in the order that worked best for the student, and lessons were often longer than would work for other kids because Drew's daughter finds frequent transitions difficult.

School-lite and Light School

Parents can tweak a system with older children, but we've had success with starting the routines of academics two weeks before the new semester. At Courtney's house, we call it "light school." Jenn's family calls it "school-lite." Drew called it a "soft launch." Sometimes, establishing this new routine is easier because it's a continuation of summer academics.

At Jenn's house, summertime school-lite means that everyone meets up at the prearranged time and Jenn reads a chapter of something aloud. Then everyone plays a board game or watches a documentary. The family has lunch during the scheduled school year time. Next, the children all do their chores at the same time. In the afternoons, the younger children nap, and the older children can do math with fewer distractions. Last, Jenn does a bit of spelling, phonics, or vocabulary, which finishes out the day. After all, it's summer, so Jenn keeps the day short and easy, but still in order.

At Courtney's house, light school means that only math and reading get done. This summer, her youngest child is practicing reading aloud, both for prosody and fluency, and maintaining skills in double-digit subtraction and addition. Her oldest child has summer reading for next autumn's AP classes and is finishing up algebra with Courtney. These days are short, but the regular habit of doing academics is helpful.

Drew's soft launch meant math, writing, and Latin, with the other subjects and some supplemental academic reading added in slowly over a period of weeks.

Sick Days

"Light school," "school-lite" or "soft launch" schedules are also helpful when you must take a sick day. Whether you're sick or your child is sick, 90% of the time, you can get some work done. Use your best judgment (we don't recommend holding the puke bucket and today's reading assignment at the same time), but there is a long way between a 104° Fahrenheit fever and a tummy ache. From flipping through flash cards to listening to an audio book while coloring as they lie on the sofa, your child can be somewhat productive. This low-key retrieval practice and exposure can be done even when the homeschooling parent is down with the flu.

Some children are frequently ill without being sick enough for hospitalization or bed rest. Courtney's youngest child has a complex, chronic illness that meant she was ill for weeks at a time throughout the school year. Eventually, Courtney decided that if she waited to do serious academics when her child was well, her child would never learn to read. So, they did academics even when her child was irritably ill. Unpleasant though it was, her child did eventually learn to read with fluency and comprehension.

Baskets, $9.99. Organization, priceless.

Another useful habit is using folders and supply baskets to keep work organized. Particularly for children (or parents) with executive functioning issues, having everything you need to do math or reading all together in a convenient place is critical. We have used many methods over the years, but it's important that you find something that works for your family.

One routine that Jenn and Courtney both share is meal planning. By the end of the day, we have neither the time nor the mental energy to figure out what to make for dinner. Instead, we make an order and shop once a week. We both use a slow cooker or pressure cooker as much as possible. Sheet pan meals from a freezer, lasagnas from a box, salads from a bag, and other hands-off meals are the way to go. Starting dinner during a mid-morning break means we get a little relief at 4:30, when we're exhausted from the day. This is a habit we've developed to make homeschooling easier for ourselves.

Practice Makes Perfect

Like a mouse with a block of cheese, nibble away at that mountain of knowledge, skills, and abilities through consistent routines that tackle small pieces of the whole every day. We frequently see gifted parents of gifted children sneer at the routine of memorization and review. "Drill and kill!" is their motto. Funny how they sneer at others acquiring knowledge they already have, or that their children can acquire almost effortlessly. Such a situation often becomes a "knowledge and its advantages for me, but not for thee" policy.

Have you ever thought about the popularity of quiz shows and games? Jeopardy exists because even adults like showing off what they know. One of the reasons children push back against academics is busy work. Memorization, recitation, and testing are all ways to show off with immediate feedback. Either you know the information, or you don't.

Children love learning information by heart. We have seen many children bursting with pride in their newly memorized knowledge. Google "'first language lessons poetry video" and you'll see children thrilled at reciting "Mr. Nobody" and Rossetti's "The Caterpillar" for the camera. For many children, reciting poetry or their times tables is their first opportunity to work hard at something and gain visible expertise. No matter what happens, nobody can take that learning away from them. In addition, gaining the skill of learning for recitation serves those students forever.

Some of the most joyous light-bulb moments spring from an encounter followed by a return. Repeating the information fuses the knowledge into your child's schema. One of the biggest mistakes a home educator can make is to forego the return, or repetition. What bores us does not necessarily bore our children. The learning process is one of slow but steady engagement with ideas. Gradually, the engagement builds to a critical point when the student acquires the idea. Repetition matters because it can deepen the engagement process.

Constant review works to counteract the forgetting curve. A German psychologist named Hermann Ebbinghaus showed that we forget new information at a predictable rate (shown as a curve), but review at regular intervals helps cement information in long-term memory, whether that's calculus, French verb forms, or the reflexes associated with driving on the left side of the road. In the homeschool, memory work and recitation are perfect for that type of review.

Morning Work

Parents who set out bowls of cereal and the remote control the night before Saturday morning cartoons well know that most children are morning people. Many families begin their day with a "morning basket." Ideas for what to put in your morning basket include, but are not limited to: a book of poetry; fine art coloring worksheets; a music CD and CD player; high-quality picture books; art cards or a coffee table art book; and flashcards for second language vocabulary, math, history, and science. (Have your child recite while you're getting caffeinated.) This is also a great time to get that occupational therapy or physical therapy practice in, whether that's a little embroidery practice for fine motor skills, shoe-tying for occupational therapy, or jumping jacks for physical therapy. Nibbling toast while your sibling recites their multiplication facts is a comfortable, predictable way to start your day for a child.

Write It Down

While all children benefit from structured homeschools with set routines, these are especially critical for children with special education needs. For example, children with autism often do better with clear guidelines and expectations. By giving them a daily morning routine, parents are increasing the chances of a day without meltdowns. Children with ADHD often have difficulty with executive functioning or making plans and goals. Morning work with repetitive daily, weekly, and monthly goals that you can mark off on a wall calendar helps them feel successful. As many as 20% of children suffer from anxiety, perhaps more so given recent events. Predictability is possibly the number one way to reduce their anxiety.

When you're down with the flu or helping a family member after surgery, having a predictable, written routine allows you to share some homeschooling responsibilities. Whether it's a teen running their kindergarten-age sibling through the alphabet song at lunch or your partner working through multiplication flashcards after dinner, sometimes you need all the help you can get. We know this from experience. For example, Courtney's retired mother sometimes helps with the homeschooling in their home by doing read-alouds and some recitation with her youngest grandchild, particularly for literature. At one point, Courtney's husband was the primary caregiver while Courtney was working two jobs, and thanks to the daily checklist, he muddled through for a few months. There is no requirement that you have to keep everything fresh and dazzling by doing it all yourself.

9 to 5 and Then Some

Jenn and Courtney both work and homeschool, so yes, it can be done. In fact, we wrote this book and homeschooled at the same time. As most US parents already know, scheduling is key with children. The juggling skills you already have as a parent can help you homeschool and work at the same time. Basically, you're pulling two shifts every day.

At one point, Jenn was a general contractor. She took the children with her on supply runs all the time. Every day had a different schedule. She learned that you want to plan your butt-in-seat work for a place where you have a chair and table. We've done academics in the car, too. A backpack prepared the night before with that day's materials and a hard-backed clipboard for a writing surface can make sure you get it done.

Another key point is that academics don't have to be done during business hours. If you're willing to be flexible, you can do algebra with your teen instead of watching the 6 o'clock news and read *How Do Apples Grow?* at bedtime. Think outside the workweek, too. Saturday and Sunday are there every week and core academics need to be done when you have time.

When you're a working parent, efficiency comes before fun, messy projects and slow afternoons cuddling on the sofa. You simply don't have time for it, no matter how attractive it seems on Instagram. This means you need to choose curricula that do the most with the least time from you. Generally, that choice will be a scripted curriculum. Even when half your mind is focused on work, the other half can follow along with a prepared lesson.

Learning From You and Others

When you have a good relationship with your child, you can often get away with asking your child to do something without too much pushback because they trust you. "Honey, read this, please." And at least six times out of ten, they'll do it. More or less.

However, your child also needs to learn from people who aren't you. Unless your family is independently wealthy (and often even then), your child will need to learn to take direction from others. Both now as a child and later as an adult, they'll need to study something they're not interested in without sass or slacking off. Whether it's bar exams or employer-based training, they'll need that experience.

One way to make sure your child has those skills is to outsource a subject. You could outsource something they're good at, to create a sense of competence and help them focus on following directions with a good attitude and follow through. Or you could outsource a troublesome area because you need help teaching your child. We've done both of these at different times, either with online classes or with face-to-face classes.

Most people don't work from home, alone all day. In a typical work environment, people need to get along in groups, large and small. While we don't think that you need to pretend that work acquaintances are your friends, your child does need to learn how to maintain socially acceptable behavior in long-term group projects. Clubs

like Girl Scouts and 4-H, athletic teams, and volunteer work all help provide this necessary skill.

Housework

You should not be doing all the housework. Your partner (if you have one) and your children can do plenty to keep the household humming along. For example, Courtney's husband handles the dishwasher and Courtney's eldest handles the laundry. At age 8, Courtney's youngest daughter is perfectly capable of setting and clearing the table and assisting with dinner. Jenn's youngest son regularly makes dinner for the whole family.

Believe it or not, there are people who do research about children doing chores. They suggest that as early as age three, children benefit from doing chores. What kind of benefits? Children who do chores are more able to handle frustration, delayed gratification, and stressful situations. In addition, children who do chores learn time management skills, organization skills, and later, how to function as an independent adult. Furthermore, they have better empathy.

You may find this discussion of housework ridiculous in a book about homeschooling, but *you will be spending the majority of your day in your home.* Obvious, yes? Less obvious is that when your home is relatively clean and organized, you'll get more done. Taking Friday afternoons or Monday mornings to do a whole-family cleaning ritual helps ensure that you are comfortable and productive in your home.

Below is a schedule of cleaning chores. While you should absolutely make sure assigned tasks are suitable for your own children, we think many items can be completed by children ages five and up. Ages 12 and up can complete all the items. Remember, housework poorly done is still done. Bite your tongue if it isn't done to your standard. If every chore time becomes criticism time, chore time will become battle time, and nobody wants that. With practice, your partner and your children will get better at it.

And if they don't? A slightly messy house is not the worst thing in the world. As long as your household is functional—your children are fed, clothed, bathed, loved, and educated—you're doing OK. What's going to matter more in 20 years: that the socks are all mated and tidied away in drawers or that your youngest child is a fluent reader? You know the answer to that question. A family sock basket and 12-packs of athletic socks are easy fixes.

If you have the funds, outsource it! Weekly cleaning and lawn maintenance may seem pricey, but think about that private school tuition that you aren't paying.

Housework Schedule		
Daily		
• Dry clothes. • Empty garbage can, take the garbage outside, and replace the bag. • Feed pets. • Fold blankets on the sofa. • Hang up coats. • Make beds. • Prepare meals. • Prepare tomorrow's clothes. • Put away clean clothes.	• Put away toys and stuffed animals. • Put dirty clothes in the hamper. • Put leftovers and other food away. • Put up clean dishes. • Put away shoes. • Put away books and magazines. • Replace soap, toilet paper, and tissues as needed. • Set and clear the table.	• Sweep/vacuum and mop as needed. • Wash clothes. • Wash the dishes, pots and pans. • Water plants. • Wipe down the sinks and tubs. • Wipe off the dining room table. • Wipe off the kitchen counters.
Weekly		
• Change the sheets. • Clean old food and spills from the refrigerator. • Dust (pictures, mirrors, light fixtures, light bulbs). • Make a weekly menu plan. • Mop dirty floors. • Order/shop for groceries.	• Scrub the kitchen sinks, counters, tabletops, and backsplashes. • Scrub the toilet, sink, tub, bathroom wall, toothbrush holders, cabinets, mirror, and floor. • Vacuum all the rugs, upholstered furniture, and lampshades.	• Wipe down doorknobs, woodwork, telephones, keyboards. • Wipe down garbage cans. • Wipe down kitchen and bathroom cabinets. • Wipe down the stove top.
Monthly		
• Wash the mattress covers, pillow covers, and blankets.		
Quarterly		
• Clean fan blades. • Clean the oven. • Dust blinds/shades and door tops. • Organize the drawers and closets.	• Replace pillows or wash and dry them. • Scrub the lampshades. • Turn mattresses. • Wash all the mirrors.	• Wash the woodwork. • Wash windows, screens.
Annually		
• Change out-of-season, or unwearable clothing out. • Clean all closets, drawers, cabinets. • Clean all walls, ceilings, and floors. • Clean and polish jewelry. • Clean attic. • Clean basement.	• Dry-clean or wash curtains/drapes. • Dust china, crystal, knickknacks. • Move and clean under appliances. • Organize/store DVD/CD/etc. • Organize household records. • Shampoo rugs and upholstery.	• Update household inventory. • Vacuum books. • Wash blankets, comforters, quilts. • Wash blinds/shades.

CHAPTER 21
KNOWING WHEN TO QUIT

Quitting is a tricky subject, and you might be surprised that we're even discussing it. But part of doing a good job is knowing when you're *not* doing a good job. Going into it with clear guidelines about when homeschooling is not working can help you ensure that you're doing a fair assessment.

Fact is, relatively few people educate all of their children from kindergarten all the way through high school. Some only homeschool for a year or two, and others set out with the intention of sending their kids to brick-and-mortar middle or high schools. Drew sent their daughter to school at various times during her school career. She attended 3rd grade at the private school where Drew taught at the time, and the family later opted to send her to the local public elementary school so she could better access special education services through the district. She graduated from a small, progressive public charter school with an excellent social curriculum and some outstanding teachers. She says that her experiences in these varied academic settings prepared her well for college, both academically and socially.

Making the Decision

Like any important decision, deciding whether to quit should be approached when you're well-rested, well-fed, and open-minded. This is not about you being a bad person, or your children being bad people. Many people love homeschooling but find that, for one reason or another, homeschooling no longer works for their  family. Plenty of people thought they would love homeschooling and then slowly realize they're overwhelmed. Both of these scenarios mean that you're human.

Home education is an immense task for anyone. You only have so many hours in the day, and you only have the children in your home. Unless you teach at Hogwarts or your name is Doctor Who, you probably can't magically bend time to create more hours in your day. Likewise, you can't exchange your children for an easier-to-educate model. As Drew says, "You can outsource schooling, but not parenting." Sometimes, parenting has to come first.

You may feel that you cannot meet all your child's needs at home, and you might be right about that. Intensive occupational therapy, dyslexia remediation, physical therapy, speech therapy, nursing care, orientation and mobility training, Braille instruction and transcription, and ASL instruction and translation are all professional services offered in public schools. Sometimes districts will allow homeschoolers to access those services, and sometimes they won't. Insurance often refuses to cover these on the basis that public schools offer them. If you don't have thousands of dollars to privately pay for those services, there's no shame in doing what's best for your child. This is the primary reason Drew sent his daughter to an otherwise mediocre public elementary school in 5th and 6th grades.

In addition, trained professional educators are, well, trained professional educators. Not every homeschooler feels like they can do as well as or better than someone with a bachelor's or master's degree and years of experience. There are millions of highly trained and qualified professional teachers who are experts at their jobs, and there is no shame in making use of their skills.

Sometimes, we find that parents forget that both homeschooling and sending your child to public school are temporary decisions. Maybe you're having a difficult pregnancy, you're utterly exhausted, and you desperately need quiet afternoons to recuperate. Sending your noisy younger children to daycare or preschool while you homeschool the quiet older children is absolutely an option. Maybe you need to send both groups for the rest of the school year so that you have the house to yourself for regular afternoon naps and time to dedicate to the new baby. That's OK too! Your choices can change in the next school year.

We've been there! Jenn has five children. Her oldest two boys started out in public school and fell behind. Jenn then tried parochial schools for them, and they weren't successful there either. (Like many people, homeschooling wasn't her first choice.) Jenn's third son was homeschooled for all of elementary school. Then, when her family moved to a new, highly rated school district, he wanted to go to public high school.

At that point, Jenn was tired. Her third son has severe ADHD and teaching him was difficult. She had two younger children who needed her time and attention as well. Her extroverted, bright boy was lucky enough to be funneled into a program where he was bused to a community college for part of the school day. This decision worked out well for him. But, public school didn't change his ADHD, and supporting him through public school took nearly as much time as homeschooling him.

Now that he's an adult, Jenn is glad she didn't feel that she had to stick with homeschooling him all the way through. Many people do feel obligated to see the commitment through and that's an understandable point of view. Might he have had more time for outside activities if he was homeschooled through high school? Maybe, but there's no point in second-guessing the decision. And you know what? He's a fully functional (medicated) adult now.

Do you feel like you are failing by considering whether to send your children to school? Here's a thought experiment: What if you drove to the store on a standard route every day? Every day you get stuck in traffic on this route. One day you realize that you could go down a different road. You'd congratulate yourself for solving a problem, not feel guilty for not sitting in traffic. In the same way, don't get "stuck" in homeschooling when you could solve the problem by sending your child to school.

Good questions to ask yourself about quitting include:

- **Why are you homeschooling?**

  Maybe your child urgently needed intensive professional assistance, but now they're not in crisis anymore. That's great! School is right there and might be good for your child.

- **If you're homeschooling because of COVID or poor public schools, has the situation changed?**

  Maybe COVID has receded, your local public schools are wide open, and no one in your household is immunocompromised. Now is a great time to send your children to school. Maybe you've moved to a better district or won a lottery admission to a magnet school. Take advantage of the changed situation without guilt.

- **Do you have time to homeschool?**

  Yes, you *can* be flexible while homeschooling, but you shouldn't be flexible at your own expense—or your child's. If you're perpetually missing important deadlines, irritable because the house is always a mess, and finding your child behind in reading or math, then the change you need to make might be putting your children in a school or daycare. After all, you can't get water from an empty well.

- **Do you feel like you're stuck?**

  No one should be home educating out of guilt or obligation. (Obvious caveat: worldwide plague, but we hope those are rare.) So what if you hear a few "I told you so!" comments? We're all trying to do the best we can for the kids we have, and when their needs change, our methods also need to change.

- **Do you feel like no one understands how much you do all day every day?**

  First, we do understand! Go you! You're the best. Secondly, teaching from a state of resentment is not great for you or your kids. If doing it all yourself is too much and you want to keep your kids at home, go for the minimalist approach. Focus your efforts on short daily lessons in reading, writing, and math, because you can't get blood from a stone.

  Better yet, outsource as much as possible. Can you swap days of the week with a friend? They take all the kids Monday/Wednesday, you take them Tuesday/Thursday, and everybody takes Friday off. Maybe you could join 4-H and have your child use their 4-H project as their science this year. Is there a co-op nearby that teaches history? Let someone else take charge of as much as you can stand. Some years are like that.

- **Have you tried to meet your children's needs to the best of your ability but everyone is still miserable?**

  Time to try something else. Misery is not a requirement for raising children. Neither is being unhappy a regular feature of childhood. Let yourself put your unhappy child in the hands of a professional educator for seven hours a day. Find what sparks joy in your life and cultivate it, whether it's joining a romance book club at the library or finally finding the time to get away for a weekend with friends.

We're not discouraging people from homeschooling, but we recognize that homeschooling is a major life decision that requires serious consideration. Parenting doesn't have to be an arms race, and homeschooling doesn't have to be a cruise missile in your arsenal. If you're miserable, resentful, guilty, and exhausted, the children and everyone else in your household can tell. And you know what they say: "Put on your own oxygen mask first." Life is too short to be unhappy.

EPILOGUE

Remember our fictional homeschoolers from chapter 1? We're revisiting them here to show some different possible homeschooling outcomes. We want to remind you that, with the exception of Jenn's daughter's story, these scenarios are composites of situations we've seen in our professional lives, not real individuals, but we hope that seeing the range of experiences will help you envision and plan for your own home education journey. We wish you good luck and happy homeschooling!

The Accidental Homeschooler

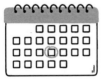

Mary, whose husband was frequently deployed overseas for months at time, found that she enjoyed homeschooling her boys. As she expected, she had a lot of support from other military families in the area. With all the social outlets provided by other military families and local homeschooling groups, her children are doing well emotionally. However, Mary also discovered that her older son is gifted and she found it increasingly hard to give him the academic challenge he needs. When Mary's husband was transferred to an area with an excellent magnet school for STEM—her older son's strength—the family decided he will attend while the younger child continues to homeschool. Mary is grateful that she has options that allow her to meet each child's needs.

The Pandemic Homeschooler

Dawn and her mother, Cindy, are glad they chose to homeschool Dawn's three children. Virtual schooling hadn't been a good fit, but thanks to Grandma Cindy's efforts while Dawn was working the night shift, the children are all working at grade level. The children have enjoyed having a closer relationship with their grandmother and grandfather, and Dawn's new job has helped with the household's bottom line. Cindy is willing to continue as the primary homeschool teacher for at least another year, but the family is holding open the possibility that the children will return to school after that year. In the meantime, Dawn is looking for a job that will allow her to support the kids on her own.

The Unhappy Homeschooler

Alicia's child, who'd had such a difficult experience at school, has blossomed at home. Without the constant stress of poorly disciplined peers and dubious academics, his willingness to work on his studies has improved. Thanks to their son's new study skills and better attitude, Alicia and her husband feel like they have their sweet boy back again. With Alicia's support, he has branched out into many extracurricular activities, both online and offline. Locally, he's found a niche volunteering at the local pet shelter and is thinking about going to veterinarian school. Online, he became good friends with some other teens in an online Minecraft club. Over the summer, he plans to travel to visit one of them.

The Medical Needs Homeschooler

It hasn't always been easy for Tanya to shuttle her daughter back and forth to so many medical treatments, but their church family has come through with a meal train, and fellow homeschoolers have loaned her scripted curriculum that's easy for her to teach in small chunks between appointments.
As she'd hoped, Tanya's local homeschooling group helped her daughter keep learning Spanish through weekly pod meetings. In addition, Tanya and her daughter make a point of listening to audiobooks in the car on the way to and from appointments. Tanya knows the road ahead will be rough as her daughter's medical conditions continue, but she's looking forward to making sure her child stays with her peers in terms of academics so that her daughter can eventually return to school.

The Academic Homeschooler

After a difficult start, Rachel and her wife realized that their son was profoundly gifted. With her uncle's help, Rachel learned how to meet her son's academic needs at home. Unlike her uncle's past experience, Rachel found that they now have many choices for outsourcing with online classes. With advice from a Facebook group for the parents of gifted children, she's  managed to find some great experiences for her son. Rachel has even been in touch with the local community college, and while her son is too young to enroll, a few teachers have agreed to let him audit their classes. Rachel is already researching dual enrollment options for high school, and she feels confident that they will be able to guide him through an excellent education.

The Special Education Homeschooler

After receiving Mia's diagnosis of autism and ADHD, Eric and his wife knew they'd need to educate themselves so they could meet her needs while homeschooling. They read books, listened to podcasts, searched on social media, and reached out to local homeschool groups with many neurodiverse families. After a year of homeschooling, Eric wasn't sure whether Mia or he had learned more! That year was difficult, with a lot of trial and error to find curricula and a schedule that worked  for Mia. There were some late nights for Eric and some meltdowns from Mia along the way. But with the help of medication and a supportive educational psychologist, Mia is thriving at home, cheerful and bubbly once again.

The Aspiring-Pro Child Homeschooler

After a long conversation with her daughter, Lucy decided to grant Olivia's fervent wishes and begin the homeschooling process on a trial basis. Lucy wasn't sure how well Olivia was going to balance her pre-professional dance program with evenings spent on academics, but Olivia rose to the challenge. Leaning on the other parents who were also homeschooling children enrolled in the program, Lucy found a schedule that worked for them both. By focusing on the core subjects and using straightforward, scripted curricula, Lucy was assured that Olivia was getting the education she needed while giving her the necessary time to pursue her dancing dreams.

The Religious Homeschooler

With their overseas missionary work coming to a close, Sarah and Michael were busy preparing to return to the United States. Because Sarah had taken on the primary responsibility to homeschool using tightly scheduled rigorous curricula, all of their children were well-prepared to enter the private, religious school that Sarah and Michael had both attended. The children passed the entrance exams  with flying colors, and Sarah and Michael began thinking about how their lives would change as the older children transitioned back to school.

The Intentional Homeschooler

Although they had planned to homeschool their daughter, Abigail, all the way from kindergarten through 12th grade, Jakob and Esteban discovered that she was a vivacious extrovert who needed more social interaction than they could provide in their local community. Even though they'd made sure to spend time outdoors with local groups every week, they realized that Abigail needed hours every day with other children to be happy. The couple heard  about a new Spanish immersion charter school in the next town and put Abigail's name into the admissions lottery. She was accepted and is thrilled at the prospect of making new *amigos y amigas* next year.

The Afterschooling Homeschooler

After a long discussion with her husband, Elizabeth swallowed her doubts and spent the money on the expensive reading curriculum she'd heard about online. Elizabeth followed the instructions exactly, tutoring Bobby in reading every day after school. Despite his protests about doing more homework, Elizabeth was thrilled when the end of year school exams  showed that Bobby was reading at grade level. Elizabeth realized, however, that reading instruction was not the only thing lacking in the boy's school. Boosted by his success and delighted by their deepening relationship, Elizabeth decided she would try homeschooling him for a year while she researched other educational options. Who knows what the future might bring?

Jenn's Daughter's Homeschool Review

As a teenager, the biggest compliment someone could give me was "You were homeschooled?! But you're so normal!" Those comments were validating because I had spent most years of my childhood filled with anxiety that I would never be able to "fit in." I worried I would miss out on key social events that the school system provided, that I would never be able to catch up.

But, after some time in college I found myself enjoying the structure even more than my public schooled peers. They had years of accumulated school fatigue, making their work difficult. I found myself excited to conquer the challenge of college. I worked hard and graduated at the top of my class, alongside a group of the most loving and supportive friends I've ever had.

APPENDICES

APPENDIX A: HOMESCHOOLING LAWS

It is vital that home educators know and follow their local laws. Although the information below was current at the time of writing, laws do change, so we urge readers to visit their locale's Department of Education website for up-to-date information.

State	Options	Ages	Notification	Mandated Assessments	Mandated Subjects
Alabama	3	6-17	Yes	No	No
Alaska	4	7-16	No	No	No
Arizona	1	6-16	Yes	No	Yes
Arkansas	1	5-17	Yes	No	No
California	3	6-18	Yes	No	Yes
Colorado	3	6-17	Yes	Yes	Yes
Connecticut	1	5-17	No	No	Yes
Delaware	3	5-16	Yes	No	No
Florida	3	6-16	Depends	Depends	No
Georgia	1	6-16	Yes	Yes	Yes
Hawaii	2	5-18	Yes	Yes	No (other)
Idaho	1	7-16	No	No	Yes
Illinois	1	6-17	No	No	Yes
Indiana	1	7-18	No	No	No
Iowa	5	6-16	Yes	Sometimes	Sometimes
Kansas	1	7-18	Yes - (1st year only)	Yes	No
Kentucky	1	6-18	Yes	No	Yes
Louisiana	2	5-18	Yes	Sometimes	Sometimes
Maine	2	6-17	Yes	Sometimes	Yes

State	Options	Ages	Notification	Mandated Assessments	Mandated Subjects
Maryland	4	5-18	Yes	No	Yes
Massachusetts	1	6-16	Yes	Yes	Yes
Michigan	2	6-18	Sometimes	No	Yes
Minnesota	1	7-17	Yes	Yes	Yes
Mississippi	1	6-17	Yes	No	No
Missouri	1	7-17	No	No	Yes
Montana	1	7-16	Yes	No	Yes
Nebraska	1	6-16	Yes	Yes	Yes
Nevada	1	7-18	Yes	No	Yes
New Hampshire	1	6-18	Yes	Yes	Yes
New Jersey	1	6-16	No	No	No
New Mexico	1	5-18	Yes	No	Yes
New York	1	6-17	Yes	Yes	Yes
North Carolina	1	7-16	Yes	Yes	Yes
North Dakota	2	7-16	Yes	Yes	Yes
Ohio	2	6-18	Yes	Yes	Yes
Oklahoma	1	5-18	No	No	No
Oregon	1	6-18	Yes	Yes	No
Pennsylvania	4	6-18	Yes	No	Yes
Rhode Island	1	6-18	Yes	No	Yes
South Carolina	3	5-17	No	No	Yes
South Dakota	1	6-18	Yes	No	Yes
Tennessee	3	6-17	Yes	No	No
Texas	1	6-18	No	No	Yes
Utah	1	6-18	Yes	No	No
Vermont	1	6-16	Yes	Yes	Yes
Virginia	4	5-18	Yes	No	No
Washington	2	8-18	Yes	Yes	Yes
West Virginia	3	6-17	Yes	Yes	Yes
Wisconsin	1	6-18	Yes	No	Yes
Wyoming	2	7-16	Yes	No	Yes

B: SAMPLE LESSON PLAN AND CURRICULUM EVALUATION CHECKLIST

Lesson #: Title

Key Question/Objective

Materials
- inexpensive
- kits available
- minimum of parts
- workbooks & textbooks

Retrieval Practice (flashcards pre-printed)
- a question from last week (answer provided)
- a question from last month (answer provided)
- a question from last term (answer provided)

Pre-requisite Knowledge Check
- **Statement** (Questions and answers provided)
- **Vocabulary.** Ask students to define via quick written activity. (matching, multiple choice, fill-in-the-blanks) Minimal writing required.
- **Concepts.** Students could summarize, list procedure steps orally, complete chart with blank labels, etc.
- **Error check.** Review major mistakes from previous lessons. Ask students to recite correct information and/or confirm good understanding of key points.

Notes:
- explanation of why this knowledge is important
- scribe when necessary

Lesson

1. Reiterate **current student understanding.** Confirm student understanding.
2. **Add new idea.** Clarify how this is different from Step 1 with a visual display. Ask students to restate.
3. Provided a **specific example**, step-by-step, with a narrated drawing built up from a blank board. Review the final product, asking students to ID each step. "And then?"

Notes:
- Present new information in small chunks. Check for understanding at each step.
- Model the analysis out loud.

4. Provide a **series of examples** and require a check for understanding with each one. Explain each step as examples are worked to provide student support.
   a) *general rule* example
   b) *exception* to the rule / special case example
   c) *common mistake* non-examples
5) **Guided Practice** (students should correctly complete at least 4 of 5 questions)
   a) Observe students completing skill/knowledge practice. Correct as needed.
   - script questions that require students to summarize, elaborate, and rephrase
   - ask students with errors to repeat directions to help identify errors
   b) Provide scaffolds for independent work.
   - written step-by-step directions
   - graphic organizers
   - exemplar pieces of work
   - mnemonics
6) **Independent Practice** (20% new / 80% review)
   a) same as guided practice
   b) interleaved problems/questions/tasks
   c) interval spaced with prior learning

Notes:
- To avoid overwhelming students, never just show entire drawing. Always build it.
- This is time intensive. Prepare more examples than students will need, just in case.
- Refer students to scaffolds as you observe.
- Fluency is the goal.

drawing example for instructor

201

Curricula Checklist

Evaluation Standards - Level 1

- author subject matter expertise (degrees, work experience, publications)

- curriculum has been field-tested by non-family members

- curriculum is designed for non-gifted students

Evaluation Standards - Level 2

- Has pacing guide

- Has sample answers for all questions

- Has prompts/teaching notes for you

- Has interleaved, interval-spaced problem sets/questions

- Professionally designed assessments (formative and summative)

Evaluation Standards - Level 3

- Fits your long-term plan

- Better than current curricula

- Has scripts

- Open-and-go usability

- Identifiable strengths and weaknesses

- Good education philosophy match

- You can stand the graphic design

- Your child meets the level's pre-requisites

- Has a scope and sequence

- Contains good lesson plans

- Usable for neurodivergent homes

Evaluation Standards - Level 4

- prerequisite knowledge checks in lessons
- deliberate linking to prior knowledge
- detailed instructions and assignments
- simple, concrete instructions
- examples and non-examples in lessons
- useful, simple pictures and graphs
- 80/20 old information/new problem practice split
- detailed rubrics for successful assignments, not above/middle/below
- assignments divided into small chunks
- frequent (at least weekly) quizzes
- time expectations for assignments
- extra practice for difficult areas
- low distraction black and white

RECOMMENDED READING

- *The Knowledge Deficit: Closing the Shocking Education Gap for American Children.* Hirsch, E. D. (2006). Boston: Houghton Mifflin.
- *Why Don't Students Like School? A Cognitive Scientist Answers Questions about How the Mind Works and What It Means for the Classroom.* Willingham, D. T. (2009). Jossey-Bass.
- *Make It Stick: The Science of Successful Learning.* Brown, P. C., Roediger, H. L. III, & McDaniel, M. A. (2014). Boston: Belknap Press.
- *The Knowledge Gap: The Hidden Cause of America's Broken Education System—and How to Fix It.* Wexler, N. (2019). New York: Avery.
- *Language at the Speed of Sight: How We Read, Why So Many Can't, and What Can Be Done about It.* Seidenberg, M. S. (2017). New York: Basic Books.
- *The Number Sense: How the Mind Creates Mathematics.* Dehaene, S. (2011). Oxford University Press.